LANDSCAPING

with *WOOD*

LANDSCAPING
with *WOOD*

THE PRACTICAL GUIDE TO BUILDING OUTDOORS

SCOTT MCBRIDE

The Taunton Press

Taunton
BOOKS & VIDEOS
for fellow enthusiasts

Printed in the United States of America
10 9 8 7 6 5 4 3 2 1

The Taunton Press, Inc., 63 South Main Street,
PO Box 5506, Newtown, CT 06470-5506
e-mail: tp@taunton.com

Distributed by Publishers Group West

Library of Congress Cataloging-in-Publication Data

McBride, Scott.
     Landscaping with Wood / McBride.
       p.   cm.
     Includes bibliographical references and index.
     ISBN 1-56158-194-1
      1. Garden structures—Design and construction. 2. Wooden fences–
Design and construction—Amateurs' manuals. 3. Trellisses—design and
construction—Amateurs' manuals. 4. Landscape architecture—Amateurs'
manuals. I. Title.
     TT4961.M377   1999
      624–dc21   98-44061
                                                          CIP

About Your Safety
Working with wood is inherently dangerous. Using hand or power tools improperly or ignoring standard safety practices can lead to permanent injury or even death. Don't try to perform operations you learn about here (or elsewhere) unless you're certain they are safe for you. If something about an operation doesn't feel right, don't do it. Look for another way. We want you to enjoy the craft, so please keep safety foremost in your mind whenever you're working with wood.

For Nancy

Acknowledgments

First I would like to thank my old pal Kevin Ireton for nominating me to write this book. Over the years he has done as much as anyone to turn a ranting carpenter into a technical journalist. Other contributors to that process were Mark Feirer, John Lively, and many others.

I have been shepherded through my first book by three expert ladies. Helen Albert helped me hammer out a vision for the book and kept faith in me despite several false starts. Thanks, Helen. Cherilyn DeVries kept the effort chugging along and held my hand through several bouts of computer hysteria. The lion's share of the job went to Jennifer Renjilian. Working on a skin-tight schedule, she managed to rope in my unruly manuscript with care and sensitivity. I wish to thank Holly Pendleton, Roe Osborn, and Rita Meyers for coaching me on computers, and Steve Dudley for his advice on photo equipment. I would like to thank *someone* for telling me how to take good pictures, but I have finally concluded that nobody can do that except the merciless camera. Chuck Miller came the closest when I begged him for a few morsels of photo wisdom. "You'll do fine, kid," he said. "You've got the eye."

Thanks to my brother in faith John A. Jenkins for his recommendations on paths—the garden variety as well as the spiritual kind. Special thanks to master builders Peter Kreyling and Kevin Weisgerber for sharing their knowledge of retaining walls. Thanks also to landscape designers Brendan Foster and Elizabeth Martin for their expertise on garden matters.

I'm indebted to my photo models Kevin, Nan, Ryan, and Terry for their patience ("Just hold that oak beam up for *one more minute…*") and to the many people who let a complete stranger walk into their yards to take pictures.

Thanks to my parents Al and Barbara McBride, who taught me to love beautiful books as well as beautiful homes. Finally, a special word of appreciation to my high school shop teacher, Mr. Joe Tibbs, wherever you are. Your encouragement meant so much.

Contents

Introduction

There's a little bit of woodworker in every gardener, starting with the first twig used to skewer a seed packet. I began building wooden structures for our family garden 20 years ago. I didn't know much about horticulture or carpentry, but my ignorance was superseded by my enthusiasm. Consequently, I made my share of mistakes. I built retaining walls with untreated barn timbers that rotted after a season. To make arches, I joined wooden segments with plywood splines; the plywood speedily delaminated. The 2x4 borders around our vegetable bed heaved because of inadequate drainage, and our impatiens languished in too-shallow planters I built. One day the building inspector even showed up to inform me that the 400 ft. of scrolled picket fence I had just built around our property was a foot too high.

The craftsman in me was chagrined by these failures, but the knowing farmer inside just shrugged. After all, disappointment is a perennial visitor to any adventuresome gardener who knows that this year's disaster lays the foundation for next year's bumper crop.

Success in my endeavors often was as unexpected as my failures—the grapevine that covered the arbor I built in just two years, the trellis that cast eerie shadows by night when a lantern was placed inside. Encouraged by the victories, I continued to adorn our little Eden. Eventually the place began to teeter dangerously on the brink of looking like a miniature theme park, plunked down mysteriously on a suburban side street.

Carpentry eventually became my career, while gardening remained a hobby. Though my enjoyment of woodworking has evolved as my skills and tools have grown, I have rarely again experienced the thrill of seeing those early garden structures pop up in the landscape. Unencumbered by the finicky tolerances of indoor carpentry, and without a client to please, I was free to conjure up a design and execute it in a single Saturday. Wood, by its moderate cost and yielding nature, was the perfect material for such impulsive escapades. More often than not, the results were satisfying. In the season that followed, I watched with pleasure as my creations posed against the shifting backdrops of summer verdure, autumn color, and winter white.

Landscaping with Wood starts at the beginning of the building process with inspiration and design ideas so you can design a structure suited to your own needs. You'll learn how to choose materials that will endure. And once you know the basics, you'll learn the nuts and bolts of garden woodworking, from foundations and framing to finishes.

But the heart of the book deals with the structures themselves, from simple borders to more involved projects like arbors and trellises. You'll learn general building guidelines for each type of structure included in these chapters, and each project is accompanied by a step-by-step photo essay, illustrating how to build a basic example of each structure.

It is my hope that *Landscaping with Wood* will spare you some of my painful mistakes and point the way to garden structures that embody those much sought-after virtues of good building: firmness, commodity, and delight.

1

Why Landscape with Wood?

It's hard to imagine a more accommodating material than wood. North America's abundant forests make wood both affordable and readily available throughout the United States and Canada. With proper forest management, wood is the ultimate renewable resource.

THE FRIENDLY BUILDING MATERIAL

Perhaps wood's greatest attraction is its workability. For one thing, wood is relatively light, making it easy to transport and erect. The strength-to-weight ratio of wood is so high that the stuff can be used to build airplanes. As building materials go, wood is also soft. There's a substantial difference between even the hardest of woods and the steel tools and fasteners used to fashion it. This is not the case with other materials. For instance, stone is only slightly softer than hardened tool steel, which makes stonecutting an arduous, drawn-out process. The same is true of metalworking. Having even a little experience with these stubborn materials will make you appreciate the ease with which a sharp sawblade will slice through a 6x6 timber.

And yet, in spite of wood's softness, it is stiff. The strength of wood is most evident in free-spanning members such as floor beams and roof rafters. Metal also has this kind of spanning strength, but it's not as attractive as wood, and masonry has practically no spanning strength. Of course, stone has great compressive strength (the ability to withstand crushing forces) but so does wood. Timber can be stacked into structures such as retaining walls and stairs in much the same way that stones or bricks are laid up in masonry, at a fraction of the weight.

Wood also has a trait that is conspicuously absent from metal: visible grain. One piece is never quite identical to another, which allows wood to blend into a living landscape more readily than homogenous materials such as metal or plastic. Wood also weathers in a way that adds to its appearance. The patina of weathered barn boards is easy to warm up to, but rusted iron and cracked plastic are hard to like.

This gate provides
a bold focal
point for a rural
landscape.

Although the natural look of raw timber is perfect for many garden settings, there may be times when a change of color is desired. In those cases, wood holds paint and stain well by virtue of its porous surface. Metal, on the other hand, requires meticulous surface preparation and special primers. (Galvanized steel is particularly troublesome to paint.) Plastic won't accept finishes at all, so you're stuck with the original color. The porosity of wood also allows it to be glued effectively, and the new generation of one-part waterproof adhesives makes glue a practical choice for outdoor woodworking.

Until recently, wood suffered from one great drawback as a material for landscaping: It rots. The only way to avoid (or reduce) this problem was to use a naturally decay-resistant species such as redwood. Beginning in the 1930s, however, researchers developed methods of forcing salt compounds deep into wood's cellular structure–a process known as pressure treatment. Today, PT (pressure-treated) wood is guaranteed for up to 30 years, but actual life spans may exceed that. PT test stakes driven

into the ground in the 1950s are still going strong. PT lumber is no more difficult to work with than untreated wood of the same species. And despite extensive testing, PT lumber has been found safe in terms of worker safety and soil contamination, as long as basic precautions are observed.

WOOD AND STYLE

Wood is extremely flexible. Large, bulky timbers can do the job of masonry, and slender beams can soar through space like steel. This has led folk builders and professional designers alike to adapt wood to every imaginable building style, from the vernacular to the grandiose.

You can adapt wood in the same way to express your vision of the landscape. If you imagine a barely tamed wilderness beyond your doorstep, you can use wood in its natural state–round, shaggy, and irregular–to edge woodland paths or to build a teahouse. If, on the other hand, you have well-ordered domesticity on your mind, you can bring all the myriad tricks of the wood artificer to bear: Wood can be planed, scroll-sawn,

A border of rail-road ties is an effective boundary between a lawn and a planting bed.

turned (on a lathe), even molded. Then it can be stained or painted to harmonize with the surrounding landscape and buildings. Paint can also be used for contrast. White is especially effective for making a structure pop out against a landscape, and it provides a contrasting foil for blossoms and greenery.

With such flexibility at your fingertips, how do you decide what to build? The recent surge of interest in all things horticultural has caused landscape structures to sprout up everywhere. The bland "turf-scape" of post–World War II America has matured, with homeowners seeking a more expressive, personalized environment. While such evolution is laudable, it's important not to get carried away by the "building bug." Observe the old design mandate "form follows function," and you'll not go wrong. If you build the structures that are truly needed for an accessible, integrated landscape, the results are likely to be both practical *and* beautiful.

WOODEN STRUCTURES: A PALETTE OF CHOICES

The design of garden structures is flexible. Many of the best examples are quirky, one-of-a-kind creations that defy classification. As a jumping–off point, however, it's useful to look at the basic types of wooden landscape structures and the functions they serve.

Borders create boundaries between such natural elements as beds, turf, meadow, and woodland. Visually, this demarcation assists the eye in "reading" the landscape. On a practical level, borders help a gardener manage the scheme by clearly defining territory and creating physical barriers to the intermingling of plant species.

Steps allow safe and easy passage from one level to another. They can also prevent erosion by terracing a sloped path into a succession of level surfaces.

Retaining walls are similar to steps but on a wider scale. They also prevent erosion and make the garden more accessible by creating a succession of level terraces in place of a single sloping surface.

A **raised bed** is a specialized form of the retaining wall. A raised bed filled with enriched soil can produce a bountiful harvest in a small footprint and can add an interesting vertical dimension to an otherwise flat site. A raised bed is also easy to cultivate because you don't have to bend over far to rake soil or to pull weeds. What's more, a raised bed provides excellent drainage even when filled with heavy soil.

The soil used to fill a raised bed can be imported from another site or can be built up from scratch by composting directly in the bed for several years before planting.

A fence of rustic timbers harmonizes with this wooded setting.

Raised beds produce a maximum yield in a minimum amount of space. They can also add a vertical dimension to a flat site.

Retaining walls turn a sloped site into a succession of level terraces. The wall on the right is made of railroad ties. The wall on the left is made of pressure-treated timbers.

Fences promote privacy among neighbors and make a strong statement of ownership. In rural settings, fences are used extensively to contain livestock.

Fences come in a bewildering array of styles. The more rustic the setting, the more naturalistic the fence should be. At the edge of a forest, for instance, a fence of peeled poles or split rails would be suitable. No finish would be applied, allowing the wood to acquire a weath-ered appearance.

Fences situated closer to buildings, on the other hand, should respect their architectural context. A clapboarded townhouse, for instance, might call for a formal picket fence with ball-topped posts and a bright white paint job.

The terms trellis, arbor, and pergola are often used interchangeably, depend-ing on whom you talk to. The problem of labels is exacerbated by the amazing variety of structures and the gardens they adorn. The following definitions are offered for the purposes of this book, although the distinctions put forth here are often blurred in practice.

A **trellis** is a light framework used to support a vine or a climbing shrub. Though a trellis is often fastened to a building for support, other types are freestanding, such as those used in a

The elegant formality of a house in town extends to this fence along the street.

This trellis helps support a climbing shrub as it scales a brick wall.

An arbor delicately punctuates the transition from street to front yard. Notice how its subtle arch rhymes with the decorative tracery over the front porch. (Designer/builder: Lawrence Dreschler.)

The pergola in this yard is carefully situated to draw the eye to a topiary arch beyond. (Designer/builder: Scott McBride.)

vegetable garden to support cucumbers and tomatoes. A trellis should be strong enough to support a sopping wet vine in full leaf yet delicate enough to blend gracefully with a winter landscape.

An **arbor** is an effective way of announcing a transition from one space, such as the street, to another space, such as the front yard. Although the skeletal form of a well-executed arbor needs no further adornment, an arbor is often used to support flowering vines and shrubs. The thicker the greenery that encompasses the arbor, the greater the sense of mystery about what lies beyond it.

A **pergola** is a more substantial cousin of the arbor. As such, it can stand on its own in a remote part of the landscape or be as close as a backyard patio. Whereas an arbor serves as a passageway, a pergola is more of an outdoor room. It often contains seating, which encourages people to pause and take in the view. The pergola also acts as an important focal point when viewed from a distance.

The views through a pergola or from within a pergola are special. To exploit this dramatic potential fully, a pergola should be situated carefully. Site the structure to take advantage of any potential focal points, such as a sundial or a special tree. After picking a likely location, construct a simple mockup. Drive poles or saplings at the corners, and then stand back for a look. From inside the mockup, try to visualize each view during each season. Move the poles around until you've found the best position.

With these structures in mind, you can develop a laundry list of desirable projects for your landscape. Let's take a hypothetical walk through your yard.

WHAT STRUCTURES DO YOU NEED?

It's the first Saturday in March, the weather is cold but sunny, and you can feel your sap rising. Clutching a coffee cup, you venture out like the proverbial groundhog, determined to map out your strategy for the coming season.

First you notice that a ragged path has developed in the lawn between your garden shed and the vegetable plot. Edging the path with 4x4 timbers and filling in between with mulch or gravel will neatly express the relationship between the building and the garden and will help to clean the soles of your boots as you exit the vegetable patch.

On one side of your property, a hillside tumbles down rather precipitously from an adjoining woods. Every time you cultivate this hillside, ruts develop from the heavy summer rains in your area. By terracing the hillside with timbers, you can solve the problem.

At the back of your lot, you're confronted with your neighbor's interesting collection of spare tires and leftover building materials. One day you see him out there changing the oil in his El Camino, so you delicately propose to him that a stockade fence would offer you both some immediate privacy.

Finally, your dining-room window faces west across a meadow. You've always enjoyed the view at sunset, but on summer evenings you would rather be sitting outside than at the dinner table. A pergola about 20 yd. from the house and a little to the left of the meadow would provide a pleasant retreat in the cool of the day. In winter, the pergola's lacy form would add interest to a bare, snowy landscape when viewed from inside.

2 Before You Build

An instructor of mine had a saying that I remind myself of whenever I'm in a big rush to start a project: "Fully planned is half done, and half planned is half baked." (The verbiage was actually a bit coarser than that.) Careful planning of any building project pays dividends in terms of less waste, fewer mistakes, and a better overall product. Good planning starts with conceiving and fine-tuning your design. But there are also practical things to consider, like building permits and estimating and ordering your materials. If well thought out, your project will go very smoothly.

FINDING INSPIRATION

Having surveyed the basic types of wooden landscape structures in the last chapter, it's time to visualize specific solutions for your site. Scour the library shelves for gardening books and magazines, and check out nurseries and home centers for brochures and project books with simple patterns.

Gardens that have been carefully thought out, such as parks, arboretums, and historic restorations, can also provide inspiration. Bring a camera along to take pictures of what you like. You might also use a tape measure and a sketch book to record the dimensions of features you particularly admire.

If you see a handsome project in your neighborhood, swallow your embarrassment and go knock on the front door. Gardeners are as vain about their accomplishments as anyone, and most will be delighted to give a tour to a friendly admirer. Ask them where they obtained their materials. If a contractor did the work, get his name and number so that you can ask him questions.

Once you have some ideas, you can begin planning your project in earnest. This involves checking out what materials are available in your area, making a photo mockup, and heading to the drawing board to make a set of plans.

Available materials

A visit to the local building supply is a good idea before sitting down at the drawing board. Wander around the place to get an idea of what's available and try to get a sense of which items are affordable and which ones will break the bank.

In the showroom you'll see all kinds of problem–solving fasteners and hardware. Premanufactured specialty items such as lattice panels and finials can enhance a design while simplifying its execution. Tell a salesperson about your project and ask them to steer you toward appropriate materials. (Mid-afternoon is the best time for lumberyard fact–finding missions; the pace slows down then, so salespeople are more indulgent.)

In the lumberyard, you can check out wood in all shapes, sizes, textures, and species. If a burly fellow comes up and asks to see your sales ticket, tell him you're just browsing. This may illicit a confused or disapproving look on his face, but ignore it—you have the right to look around.

Photo mockups

The most effective way to visualize what your landscape project will look like is to prepare a photo mockup. Begin by shooting a roll of film at the proposed building site, taking shots from different angles. A wide–angle lens is ideal for this, but a regular 50mm lens works fine. Put a person or a piece of furniture in the picture several feet from where the project will be to help you to get a handle on the scale of the project when you start to draw in the structure.

Have a set of large prints made (at least 4x6). Place a sheet of tracing paper over one of the photos and sketch in your idea. You don't need to include a lot of detail or have the right perspective; what you're mainly concerned with here is scale. Try several different sizes, even if they seem too big or too small. When you get a sense of the appropriate size, make a paper cutout and color it with colored pencils. Place the cutout on

A paper mockup can be taped or pasted onto a photo to help visualize an arbor-to-be.

the photo and slide it around until you zero in on just the right spot (see the photo above). Do the same with the photos taken from different angles.

Working drawings

Creating a set of working drawings does more than just give you a road map to follow when the chips start flying. It actually forces you to think through problems of proportion, joinery, and sequencing ahead of time. This planning gives you an opportunity to head off problems before they arise, perhaps by deciding to shift a crosspiece to a different location or by using a larger post.

Thinking in two dimensions is a talent given more to some than to others. But regardless of your level of skill with a pencil, it's worth a try. Remember, you're not trying to paint a masterpiece; you're just rehearsing the building process in a very cost–effective way. (Paper is cheap—lumber is not.) Begin with freehand sketches on cheap copy paper. Surround yourself with the photos you've found and the photo mock-ups you've made. Don't be afraid to experiment with different sizes, shapes, and details. When you've settled on a design, it's time to render working drawings to scale (see the drawing on the facing page).

A drawing board, T-square, and triangle are the draftsman's basic tools. But if you don't have a drawing board and a T-square, you can get by with just the triangle to draw all your perpendicular lines. It just takes a little longer.

To start with, you will need to settle on a scale for your drawing. For most of the projects in this book, a scale of $\frac{1}{2}$ in. = 1 ft. works well. This scale is large enough to allow you to include details but small enough to fit your drawing on a standard $8\frac{1}{2}$ x 11 sheet of paper. For a large project such as a retaining wall, you would use a smaller scale, such as $\frac{1}{4}$ in. = 1 ft. or even $\frac{1}{8}$ in. = 1 ft. For close-up details like brackets or corner intersections, you would use a larger scale, such as 1 in. = 1 ft., or simply draw them full scale (actual size).

To render measurements in the appropriate scale, an architect's rule comes in handy. It's a three-edged ruler, with different scales laid out on each edge. If you don't have an architect's rule, just use a plain ruler. If you're working in $\frac{1}{2}$-in. scale, each inch will represent 2 ft. So, if you were drawing a 6-ft. post, for instance, it would measure 3 in. on your drawing. Measurements of less than a foot can be estimated, knowing that each $\frac{1}{8}$-in. increment on the plain ruler represents one quarter of a whole foot, or 3 in.

A simple, effective way to produce scale drawings without drafting tools is to use graph paper. For small projects, I like the kind that has heavy 1-in.

squares subdivided into lighter $\frac{1}{4}$-in. squares. At a scale of 1 in. = 1 ft., the heavy squares represent feet, and the lighter squares represent 3-in. increments. This arrangement makes it easy to reference a feet/inches measurement on the drawing. At this scale, a standard $8\frac{1}{2}$ x 11 sheet of paper will accommodate projects up to 8 ft. x 10 ft.—perfect for an arbor or trellis.

OBTAINING BUILDING PERMITS AND VARIANCES

Before undertaking any major outdoor building project, call your local building department (it'll be listed in the local government section of your phone directory). Describe your project to one of the building officials, giving some idea of its size. The official also may ask for the approximate distance from the proposed project to your property line. If the project is small enough, the official may wave you ahead with no further ado. In other cases, you will be asked to apply for a permit. Localities vary widely in the stringency of their requirements, so don't assume anything.

A building permit serves several functions. First, it ensures that your project will be built according to certain minimum quality standards. For instance, your local code might require the use of pressure-treated (PT) lumber for outdoor projects. Second, a permit ensures that the structure conforms to local zoning ordinances. For instance, fences in residential zones are usually limited to a height of 6 ft. Third, if you have an architectural review board (ARB) in your locality, the permit will require that your design be reviewed. The ARB will determine whether or not your design is compatible with the prevailing architectural climate of the com-

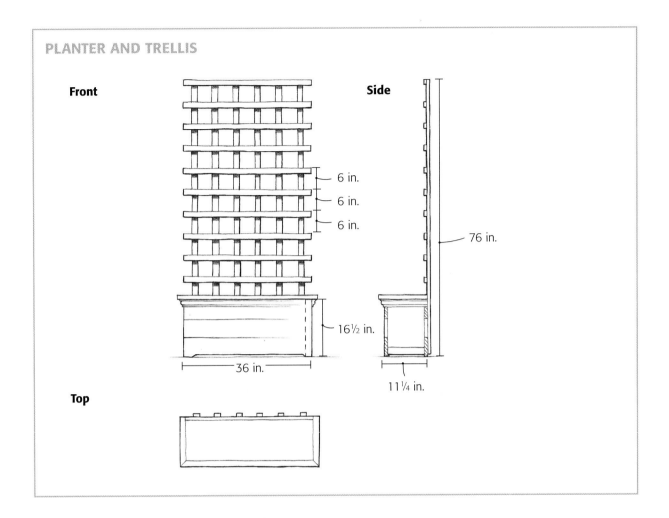

Front

Side

6 in.

6 in.

6 in.

76 in.

16½ in.

36 in.

11¼ in.

Top

munity. In some cases, the ARB will make suggestions, such as adding finials to a gate post or specifying the color of a fence. Finally, a building permit is used to adjust real estate assessments for local tax rolls. For this reason, you will be asked to show the estimated cost of construction for your project.

Although you can apply for a permit through the mail, it's quicker to visit the building department. Bring along a simple sketch of the project and a photocopy of the plot plan of your property, also called a plat. (A plat is usually attached to your property deed.) Indicate the project's location on the photocopy.

Sometimes, though, you can simply draw a thumbnail sketch of your property and show rough dimensions on it (for an example, see p. 14). For most garden projects, these simple drawings will be all that's required to file a permit application. If the officials want more detailed drawings, they'll let you know.

A building permit issued for a major structure, such as a home, will require inspections at different stages in the building process. Inspections are not usually required for the kinds of projects described in this book, but if they are, the necessary inspections will be described on the permit. For instance, if

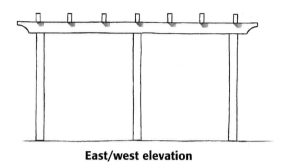

East/west elevation

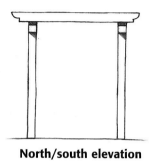

North/south elevation

Scale: ¼ in. = 1 ft.

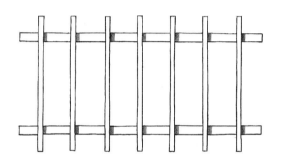

Plan view

Proposed pergola
John & Mary Stevens, owners
26 Maple Lane
Smithtown, MD 07382
(482) 607-8439

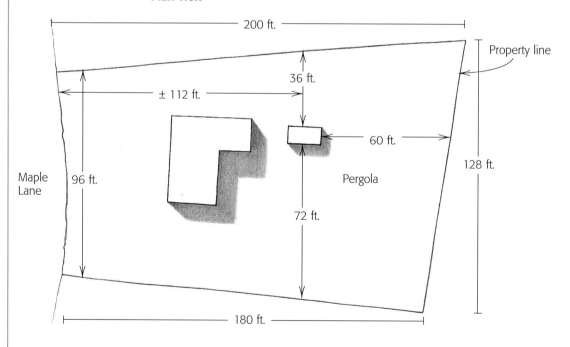

you were building a pergola, the building department might want to inspect
the depth of your post holes to make
sure they are deep enough. In that case,
you would need to call the building
department after you had dug the holes
to have them inspected by a building
official. Once the official okayed the
holes, you could proceed with the work.

Sometimes, the project you've chosen
to build may violate a local building
code. For instance, suppose you want to
build an arbor 6 ft. from your property
line, but the code in your town requires
15 ft. minimum of clearance between
such a structure and any boundary. In
such a case, you'd need a variance,
which is a special permit that allows you
to build something that would not nor-
mally be permissible under existing
ordinances. You may be required to
show hardship to have this kind of
exception made. You will also need the
consent of your neighbors.

To obtain a variance, you must apply
to the local zoning board. First, file an
application for a variance at the building
department. You'll be scheduled to
appear before the zoning board. In the
meantime, the building department will
notify your neighbors by mail that you
have made the application. They will
also be notified when the zoning board
will be considering the application.

At the meeting, you will be given an
opportunity to plead your case. In the
example mentioned above, you might
say that the arbor would provide a
much-needed privacy screen between
you and your neighbors. If none of your
neighbors object, the board may grant
the variance. If objections are raised, or
if the board feels that the variance
would set a bad precedent, the variance
may be denied.

ESTIMATING AND ORDERING BUILDING MATERIALS

Having finished a complete set of
working drawings, you should have a
good idea of the materials you'll need.
Before preparing a formal bill of materials (a builder's shopping list), simply
list the various components of the
structure on a separate sheet of paper.
Don't worry about how many or how
much at this point. You're simply making a checklist here so that you don't
overlook anything.

After completing the checklist, you
can begin the actual bill of materials
(a sample bill is shown on p. 16). Keep
it neat. On a sheet of lined paper, draw
vertical lines to produce six columns.
Start with a Quantity column, which
tells how many of a particular item
are needed, and in what units. For lumber, that would mean the number of
pieces for each length. For nails, it would
be the number of boxes and the weight
per box. (In some places, nails are sold
in bulk, so you would simply list
pounds of each size.) Many items are
sold individually, such as bolts and
framing connectors.

Next is the Item column. In this column describe the component, with as
many particulars as possible. Lumber
should be specified as to species and
grade. Nails are listed according to size
and type. Give the diameter and length
of screws and bolts. (More on these particulars in Chapter 3.)

The next column—Function—is for
your own benefit (not the salesperson's).
List the use of each component—for
instance, "legs"—so that you'll be able to
untangle the order when it's delivered. If
you plan on cutting pieces into shorter
lengths or narrower widths, note that
here as well.

SAMPLE BILL OF MATERIALS FOR ROSE ARBOR

Quantity	Item	Function	Extension	Unit price	Cost
8	1x4x8 ft. PT	Legs—outer layers			
3	1x4x8 ft. PT	Cross slats—rip to 1¾ in.	11	$1.36 ea.	$14.96
1	1x4x10 ft. PT	Legs—inner blocking	1	$1.63 ea.	$1.63
4	80-lb. concrete mix		4	$3.99 ea.	$15.95
5 lb.	6d galvanized finish nail		5	86¢/lb.	$4.30
1 lb.	1⅝ in. galvanized screw		1	$3.50/lb.	$3.50
4	1x8x8 clear cedar	Segment pieces			
1	1x8x8 clear cedar	Dogleg pieces	40	$2.75/ft.	$110.00
			Subtotal		
			Tax		
			Total		

The last three columns are where the arithmetic occurs. The Extension column is a distillation of the Quantity column. The extension is the number actually used to multiply the unit price (price per foot, pound, or whatever) to arrive at the total cost for that item. For instance, say you need two different lengths of post, eight footers and six footers. The quantity/item would be listed as 2 – 8 ft. and 4 – 6 ft., respectively. If your supplier sells 4x4 lumber by the foot, the extension would be lumped together at 40 (2x8 plus 4x6 = 40); if the supplier sells lumber by the piece, two extensions would be used (2 and 4, respectively). In another example, you might list several different sizes of bulk nails under the quantity/item columns and then combine them into total pounds under the extension column.

Confusion may arise when you present your bill of materials at the lumberyard, owing to the wide variety of pricing practices in the building materials trade. For instance, some types of lumber are priced the same per foot in all different lengths, whereas other types are sold with a premium on long lengths. In the latter case, lumber is sold by the piece rather than by the total footage. As long as your list is carefully itemized, the salesperson can work this out with you.

Once you have your bill of materials drawn up, you can put it out for bid. Fax an unpriced copy of the list to several different suppliers in your area to find the best price. Bear in mind, however, that the lowest price isn't always the best value. Verify things like delivery charges and return policies. A visit to a supplier is the best way to get a sense of the service you can expect.

Materials

Learning to build can be thought of as entering into an extended dialogue with your materials. By trial and error, they will tell you what they can and cannot do. Some of the lessons wood has to teach will appear immediately. Nail a board too close to the end, and it will split. Other lessons don't show up until after the job is done. For instance, wood that hasn't been seasoned properly may look great when you pack up your tools, but in a few weeks your perfect joints will open up as a result of shrinkage. And finally, some problems don't show up until years later. Using an easy-rotting wood such as poplar for a garden project will mean doing it over again in just a few short years.

Although lumber is the woodworker's primary medium, he or she also needs an understanding of fasteners and finishes. Fasteners such as screws and nails ensure the integrity of a project but must do so in a way that looks right. Finishes such as paint and stain have a dual role. Visually, they alter the appearance of your work to harmonize or contrast with the surroundings. On a practical level, finishes can extend the life of landscape structures by protecting them from the elements.

WOOD

Wood is a natural material full of idiosyncrasies (see the drawing on p. 18). Those idiosyncrasies are part of wood's great aesthetic appeal, distinguishing it from cold, predictable materials such as metal or plastic. At the same time, wood's "wild side" can create certain headaches for a builder. Wood contains aberrations such as knots and splits that can be thought of as defects or as character, depending on your viewpoint. Wood also has less dimensional stability than other building materials because it expands and contracts, depending on the moisture level of its environment. Finally, wood is prone to decay. Understanding these aspects of wood's personality will help you create structures that look good and perform well over the long haul.

Problems with using wood outdoors

The number one enemy of wood is moisture. Water, in the presence of oxygen, enables microorganisms to metabolize wood, causing decay. A moist environment is also hospitable to

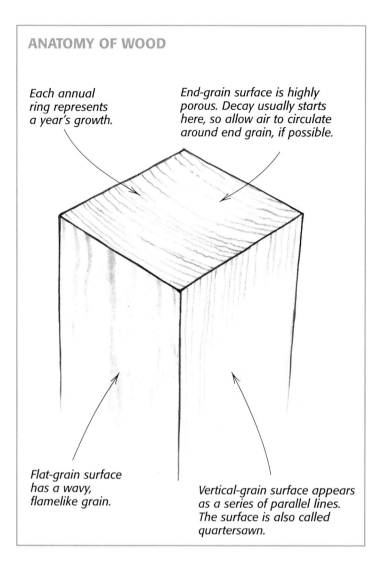

ANATOMY OF WOOD

Each annual ring represents a year's growth.

End-grain surface is highly porous. Decay usually starts here, so allow air to circulate around end grain, if possible.

Flat-grain surface has a wavy, flamelike grain.

Vertical-grain surface appears as a series of parallel lines. The surface is also called quartersawn.

wood stand in the front lines of the battle against wood decay.

Decay Wood installed outdoors in a moist climate undergoes a constant cycle of wetting and drying. Not only do rain and snow bombard the wood, but a daily sprinkling of dew also settles on its surface. More water is absorbed into the wood in some places than others, and these points are the first to start decaying. Most susceptible is end grain—the rough surface exposed when a board is cut across the grain. To promote rapid drying, structures should be designed so that as much air as possible circulates around end-grain surfaces.

Horizontal surfaces are also susceptible to wood decay. While vertical surfaces drain quickly, flat surfaces hold water by a phenomenon known as surface tension. As the water sits, it can soak through paint or water–repellent finishes (see the left photo on the facing page). To prevent this penetration, horizontal surfaces can be covered with a noncorroding sheet metal, such as copper or aluminum (see the drawing on the facing page). Another alternative is to eliminate horizontal surfaces by design. For instance, deck boards can be slightly inclined to shed water, while surfaces such as handrails and post caps can be beveled (cut on an angle).

Wood that's placed in direct contact with the ground is exposed to moisture constantly. The only effective way to fight decay in that situation is to use wood that contains natural or man–made preservatives throughout.

Unfinished wood that's exposed to intense sunlight will deteriorate into a parched, degraded state known as dry rot (see the right photo on the facing page). To protect wood from the harsh effects of sunlight, apply a finish.

wood–destroying insects such as beetles and carpenter ants. The number two enemy of wood is sunlight. Sunlight breaks down lignin, the chemical that holds wood cells together.

In the absence of these two enemies, wood can last indefinitely. Wooden objects that are thousands of years old have been found in Egyptian pyramids, preserved by the dark, dry atmosphere of the tomb. Of course, moisture and sunlight are the prime requirements for a healthy garden, so gardeners using

Exposure to strong sunlight has caused dry rot in these steps.

The decay of this column base was helped by its design. The wide horizontal surface caused water to linger, eventually penetrating the end grain of the column and the miter joints of the base. Also, no ventilation was provided to dry up moisture inside the base.

Opaque finishes such as paint or heavy stain offer the best protection. Also, the darker the color of the paint or stain, the more light it will block out.

Insects Wood decay goes hand in hand with wood–destroying insects. As the cellular structure of wood breaks down and decays, various kinds of worms and beetles move in to consume the softened material rapidly. Termites go one step further by eating sound wood as well as rotted wood. Fortunately, the same natural and man–made preservatives that repel decay also repel insects.

Almost all insect attacks start in the ground. For instance, termites tunnel up inside wooden members, leaving an

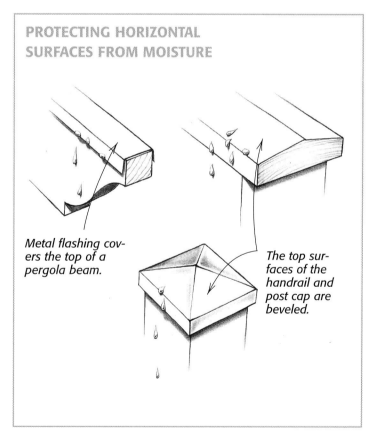

PROTECTING HORIZONTAL SURFACES FROM MOISTURE

Metal flashing covers the top of a pergola beam.

The top surfaces of the handrail and post cap are beveled.

The narrow growth rings of the board at left are characteristic of slow-grown, stable lumber. The wide-ringed board at right grew quickly and is more likely to warp.

outer shell of wood intact. They must return to the ground periodically, however, to obtain moisture. To create a line of defense, therefore, all wood that comes in contact with the ground should have a high degree of natural or man-made decay resistance. Above-ground wood of lesser decay resistance will only survive if insects are deprived of a subterranean avenue of attack.

Identifying wood defects

When lumber is sawn out of a log, it is generally straight. As the lumber dries out, it shrinks. This can cause various kinds of warping (as shown in the drawings at left). There are also natural defects in the wood to consider, such as knots, pith, and wane.

Crook and twist A board that bends along its length while remaining flat is said to be crooked, while a board that warps in three dimensions simultaneously is called twisted. Both types should be avoided. To detect these deformities in a board, pick up one end and sight down along its edge (see the drawings at left).

Crook and twist occur when natural tensions that develop in a growing tree are released by cutting and drying. More of these tensions exist in young, rapidly growing trees than in mature, slow-growing trees. Knowing this can help you avoid boards that are apt to warp as they dry. When you pick out lumber, look at the ends of the boards (see the photo above). When growth rings are tightly spaced, it means the tree grew slowly in a dark forest. These boards tend to remain stable. If the rings are far apart, the tree grew rapidly in a free-for-all with other young trees groping for light. These boards are weak and unstable.

THREE TYPES OF WARPAGE

Crooked

Looks like this from the end.

Twisted

Looks like this from the end.

Cupped

Looks like this from the side.

Cupping When a board is curved in on one face and curved out on the opposite face, it is cupped. Cupping occurs when a board shrinks more on one side than on the other. To detect cupping, sight across the end of a board or lay a straightedge across the board's face.

Splitting and checking When shrinkage occurs too rapidly, boards tend to split (see the drawing at right). The worst splitting occurs on the ends of boards, which dry out quickly as the water that's there is wicked away by evaporation. While the last few inches of the board shrink radically, the wood farther from the end remains swollen. Finally, as tension increases, the end of the board is torn apart.

Rapid drying can also cause splitting on the face of a board, usually to a lesser extent than on the ends. These defects, called face checks, often don't weaken the board structurally, but they can be unsightly. (In rustic work, the character added by moderate checking may be considered a plus.) Checks provide a point of entry for moisture, which sometimes leads to decay, especially on horizontal surfaces.

Knots, pith, and wane Knots are cylinders of hardened tissue formed in the trunk of a tree where branches are located. The way in which a board is sliced from a log dictates how a given knot will appear on the board's surface (see the drawing at right). If the face of a board is oriented perpendicular to the axis of a knot, the knot will show up as a round knot. If the face of a board cuts parallel to the knot, it will appear long and slender—a spike knot.

When selecting knotty boards, pay special attention to large, round knots. When dried rapidly, these knots may

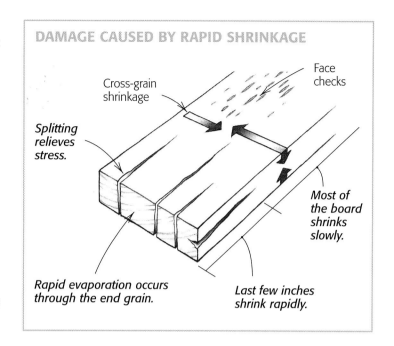

DAMAGE CAUSED BY RAPID SHRINKAGE

Cross-grain shrinkage

Face checks

Splitting relieves stress.

Most of the board shrinks slowly.

Rapid evaporation occurs through the end grain.

Last few inches shrink rapidly.

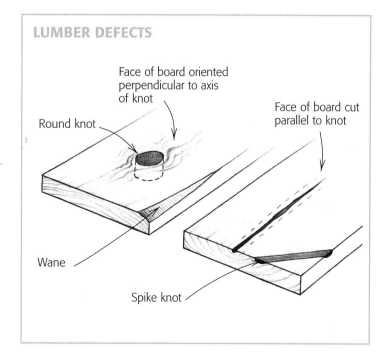

LUMBER DEFECTS

Face of board oriented perpendicular to axis of knot

Round knot

Face of board cut parallel to knot

Wane

Spike knot

become loose. If a continuous crack has developed around a knot, it is liable to fall out over time. Another problem with knots is that they contain resins that invariably bleed through paint and stain, appearing as dark shadows on the surface. The problem is especially noticeable with a light–colored finish.

Pith is the weak tissue formed in a young sapling's first few years of growth. It is found in boards cut from the very center of a log. Pith is apt to spilt and peel when exposed to the weather (see the drawing on p. 21).

Wane is an irregular absence of wood along a board's edge. It occurs when the natural outside of a log falls within the trimmed width of the board.

Whether or not you avoid these defects depends on your design intentions. If a smooth, painted surface is your goal, you should invest in clear (defect–free) boards. For rustic projects, you can save money by buying lower–

Lumber is seasoned by removing excess moisture. To promote air circulation and drying, place sticks between the boards. Cover the stack with sheets of plywood.

grade lumber, appreciating its irregularity as a token of its natural origins.

Seasoning wood

To reduce splitting and warping, softwoods should be seasoned—gradually dried until their moisture content is in equilibrium with the environment in which the wood will be used. Unseasoned lumber is said to be green, a term referring not to the actual color of the wood but to the greenness of the tree from which it was cut. Pressure-treated (PT) lumber, which is also sometimes referred to as green because of its characteristic color, may be seasoned or unseasoned. Yet a third type of green wood is that which has been harvested in an ecologically responsible way.

The moisture content of wood is expressed as a percentage of its total weight. When lumber is freshly cut, its moisture content will be 30% to 40%. If the lumber is left to dry outdoors, its moisture content will drop to about 15% in most of the United States and to about 11% in the arid Southwest. At these levels, the moisture content will stabilize, with slight fluctuations, depending on the season. Such lumber is referred to as seasoned or air–dried. You can buy an electronic moisture meter to determine the precise moisture content of your lumber, but such exactitude isn't necessary. As you work with wood, you will develop a sense of its normal dry weight. Wood that seems exceptionally heavy for a given species or that feels cold and damp to the touch is saturated with excess moisture and should be seasoned before use.

To season the wood, stack the boards in a shady place, with 1–in.–thick sticks between each layer of boards (see the photo at left). Cover the stack with plywood or sheet metal, leaving the sides of the pile exposed. The covering will keep out rain and sun. Don't cover the stack with plastic—it holds more moisture in than it keeps out. In dry summer weather, seasoning of green softwood lumber takes as little as two weeks, but in winter, it may take several months to reach moisture equilibrium.

While fresh-cut softwoods should always be seasoned, hardwoods such as oak are another story. Hardwoods tend to experience a very high degree of warping and splitting as they dry, even under ideal conditions. Once they are dry, they become so hard that they are difficult to work with. For outdoor work, it's better to use hardwoods in the green state and let them dry in place. A lot of shrinkage and a certain degree of checking will occur, but that's better than trying to work with lumber that is cupped, twisted, and hard as nails.

Some construction lumber is dried in a kiln before it is sold, and it can be used outdoors immediately. It will be marked with KD (for kiln-dried). PT lumber is dried initially, but it is then pumped full of water to convey chemical preservatives into the wood. Some PT lumber is redried after it's treated, but most of it is sold wet (which is why it's so heavy). Seasoning this saturated lumber before use greatly improves the quality of your finished product.

Choosing wood

Choosing the right type of wood for your outdoor project can be confusing. There are, after all, literally thousands of wood products available for landscape carpentry (characteristics of a few types of wood are listed in the chart on p. 24). One of your first considerations should be workability, which depends mostly on the wood's hardness. Hardwoods are more difficult to work with than softwoods, especially if you're limited to the use of hand tools. Another prime consideration is decay resistance. The two broad categories of decay-resistant lumber are those that grow naturally and those that are impregnated with preservative chemicals.

The size and shape of the material you need may restrict your choice of wood species because different trees grow in different sizes. Also, your geographical location may determine what's available locally. In some cases, technology has circumvented these restrictions by synthesizing larger and/or more durable wood products from small, nondurable trees.

Lumber can be milled in different ways. Because landscape carpentry is often massive and rustic in nature, it lends itself to the use of large beams and poles. These range from smooth-planed timbers to coarse, round logs, with many variations in between. You'll have to make a lot of decisions about what wood is best for your project.

Softwoods and hardwoods In botany, the term softwood applies to needle-bearing trees, while hardwood refers to broad-leaved trees. Most softwood trees are also coniferous (cone-bearing) and evergreen (the exceptions to the latter being cypress and larch, which shed their needles in the fall).

In carpentry, the terms hardwood and softwood refer to the wood itself. Hardwoods, such as oak, cherry, and maple, come from hardwood trees while softwoods, such as pine, cedar, and redwood, come from softwood trees. In general, wood from the softwood family of trees is softer, and thus easier to work, than hardwood lumber, but there are

WOODS FOR LANDSCAPE CARPENTRY

	Species or type	Workability	Weather resistance	Strength
Softwood (domestic)	*Redwood*	Excellent	Excellent in "all-heart" grade; moderate in grades that include sapwood	Low
	Western red cedar	Good to excellent	Excellent in "all-heart" grade; moderate in grades that include sapwood	Low
	Eastern white cedar	Easy to cut, but coarse texture	Very good	Low
	Cypress	Excellent	Excellent in heartwood; moderate in sapwood; tends to check and peel in bright sunlight	Low
	PT yellow pine, PT Douglas fir	Difficult with hand tools; good with power tools	Excellent decay resistance; sensitive to UV (ultraviolet) degradation	Good
Hardwood (domestic)	*Locust*	Difficult	Excellent	Excellent
	White oak	Difficult	Good	Excellent
Tropicals	*Ipe, greenheart, purpleheart*	Very difficult	Excellent	Excellent
	Honduras mahogany	Excellent	Good	Good
	Philippine mahogany (lauan)	Good	Good	Good
	Teak	Very difficult	Superb	Very good

exceptions. Poplar is a broad-leaved hardwood tree whose wood is almost as soft as pine, while larch is a softwood that is quite hard.

Naturally decay-resistant woods Long before man–made preservatives arrived on the scene, woodworkers observed that certain woods lasted longer outside than others. These woods, which include redwood, cedar, cypress, locust, oak, and a few tropical hardwoods, contain natural oils that inhibit decay. Most decay-

inhibiting oils are found in heartwood, which is the older, nonliving part of a tree. Sapwood is the outer wood, where sap flow occurs through living cells. Boards may contain varying amounts of heartwood and sapwood, depending on how they are cut from a log. The heart–wood, which tends to be dark in color, will usually be found at the center of a board, while the light–colored sapwood is found at the edges (see the photo on the facing page). When ordering certain species of lumber, you may be able to

Availability	Expense	Best application
Widespread, especially on West Coast	Low for construction grade; moderate for clear grade that includes sapwood; high for "clear all-heart" (CAH) grade	Construction grades: raised beds (including edibles), borders, rough fences; finish grades: arbors, trellis, pergolas, gates, fancy fences
Widespread	Moderate for construction grades; high for premium grades	See redwood
Sold mainly as manufactured items such as fence posts; raw lumber may be available in Canada and New England	Moderate	See redwood
Widespread in southeastern U.S.; hard to find elsewhere	Moderate	See redwood
Widespread for yellow pine; western states for Douglas fir	Low	Construction grades: retaining walls, raised beds (ornamentals); rough fences, borders; premium grades: arbors, trellis, pergolas, gates, fancy fences, decking
Local sawmills in eastern U.S.	Low	Fence posts, woodland steps, and borders
Widespread as a cabinet wood; sold "green" at local sawmills in Midwest and eastern U.S.	Moderate to high as kiln-dried sold at lumberyards; low as green wood sold at sawmills	Above-grade applications such as gates, fences, and decking
Importers	Moderate to high	Arbors, pergolas, gates, and decking
Importers and boat lumber dealers	Very high	See Ipe
Importers; some lumberyards	Moderate to high	See Ipe
Importers and boat lumber dealers	Out of sight	See Ipe

specify "all heart." You can also trim off the sapwood yourself for maximum decay resistance.

Redwood comes from two species: the Coast redwood, which grows along the California coast, and the Sequoia, which grows farther inland. Redwood is light, stable, and highly decay resistant. Clear, all-heart redwood that's been cut from virgin forests is available, but it's very expensive. For most outdoor projects, a grade known as "con-heart" is a good choice. Con-heart, which is cut

This redwood board contains both heartwood, which is red, and sapwood, which is cream colored. Heartwood is much more decay resistant than sapwood.

primarily from plantation-grown redwood, contains knots but no sapwood. Knots can be difficult to work around because of their hardness, but they don't affect durability. In fact, knots contain even more preservative oils than the surrounding heartwood.

Cedar has a somewhat coarser grain than redwood but still works easily. Several varieties are available in North America, but the two major groups are western and eastern cedar. Western red cedar grows primarily in Washington state and British Columbia. It has an orange to brown color. The eastern, or Atlantic, white cedar comes mostly from eastern Canada. It runs from cream to light orange in color. Western red cedar is the more decay-resistant of the two.

There are a few less-available species of cedar as well. Alaska cedar has a yellow color and a wonderful smell when it's cut. Incense cedar (an aromatic species used to line wardrobe closets) runs pink to purple in color. Because incense cedar trees are small, boards tend to be narrow and knotty. Port Orford cedar is a premium cedar prized for its fine working characteristics.

Cypress grows in the marshy areas of the southeastern United States. When virgin swamps were cut at the beginning of this century, vast quantities of wide heartwood cypress lumber—which has excellent decay resistance—were produced. Today, most of the cypress logs harvested are small in diameter and contain mainly sapwood, which has only moderate decay resistance. Sapwood is a light cream color, while heartwood is an orange-gold. A disadvantage of cypress is the tendency of its grain to peel in bright sunlight. Cypress also checks more than redwood or cedar, but for rustic garden work, these defects are not usually a problem.

Two eastern hardwoods have natural decay resistance—locust and white oak. Both of these woods are dense, hard, and difficult to work with. They're also less stable than the softwoods mentioned above. If you can find these woods at a local sawmill, however, the price can make them attractive.

Locust is a smallish tree with olive-green heartwood. It's often used for fence posts. White oak is available in large timber sizes as well as boards. The acids in white oak—called tannin—give this species its decay resistance. The same acids cause white oak to turn black when exposed to the weather.

The forests of South America, Asia, and Africa produce many tropical hardwoods with excellent decay resistance. They tend to be extremely dense, which makes them challenging to work with. On the other hand, their density can be an advantage for high-wear surfaces such as decking. A few of the better known species are ipe, greenheart, and purpleheart. Honduras mahogany and Philippine mahogany (lauan) are moderately dense tropical woods that are workable and highly stable. As a result, they're used a lot in boat building. And mahogany is more readily available than the other tropicals. As a fine cabinet wood, though, mahogany's price is steep. Teak is another fine cabinet wood. It is one of the most decay-resistant species in the world, but it is very expensive and rather difficult to work.

Both tropical and temperate rain forests are endangered by overcutting. If you're concerned about global deforestation, you can buy certified lumber products from those who manage their forests in an ecologically sound way. (For more information, see the Good Wood Alliance in Resources on p. 167.)

Pressure-treated wood Wood can also be treated with chemicals to make it resistant to decay and insects. The chemicals can be applied in either of two ways: surface treatment or pressure treatment. Surface treatment—the less effective method—is discussed with finishes (see p. 38). Pressure treatment involves forcing chemicals into wood under high pressure. The chemicals are distributed throughout the wood's entire cell structure, not just near the surface; this makes pressure treatment the most effective method of wood preserving. It's the only method recommended for wood that will be placed in contact with the ground or below grade.

Three different classes of chemicals are used in pressure treatment. The first two, creosote and pentachlorophenol (penta), are not generally recommended for residential use. At one time they were available in liquid form for field application, but they are now classified as restricted-use pesticides. Wood treated with these chemicals is still available, but it's primarily for industrial use. The third class of chemicals used for pressure treatment is salt, and the most common of these is chromated copper arsenate (CCA). Salt-treated lumber is safer and easier to use than lumber treated with either creosote or penta, and has become the standard for residential use.

Creosote is a coal-tar derivative used in the treatment of railroad ties and utility poles. Wood treated with it has a black oily appearance, and it will bleed through just about any kind of surface finish. Creosote is a skin irritant, so you should wear heavy gloves and clothing when working with this material. It should not be used for projects that will come in contact with people.

Penta is an organic chemical dissolved in oil. It's also a skin irritant and a carcinogen, so penta-treated wood should not be used for things like benches or railings. It can be used for fences and retaining walls located away from human habitation.

CCA is the most widely used chemical for pressure treatment. Two similar compounds, ammoniacal copper quaternary (ACQ) and ammoniacal copper zinc arsenate (ACZA), are also used in salt treatments.

After application, CCA reacts with wood to form an insoluble metal complex, which means the chemical will not leach out, even under wet or below-grade conditions. The amount of chemical retained in the wood after it comes out of the treatment tank determines its resistance to decay. The standard retention level for ground-contact applications is .4 lb. CCA per cubic foot of wood. Higher concentrations may be available for particularly sensitive applications such as docks and boardwalks. To be sure you're getting what you've

Buyer beware. Not all PT lumber is the same. The early failure of these 6x6s suggests that their CCA-retention level was inadequate.

The Safety of CCA-Treated Wood

The growing use of CCA-treated lumber over the last 30 years has raised concerns about safety. (After all, arsenic—one of CCA's principal ingredients—is famous as a poison.) To explore these concerns, studies have been done on workers exposed to occupational levels of CCA-treated sawdust. A 1976 study looked at carpenters in Hawaii, where large amounts of CCA-treated lumber are used

The safety of pressure-treated lumber has been questioned for more than 25 years.

as a defense against a particularly voracious termite found there. The study found no difference between the health of those workers and the health of workers who had left the trade before the introduction of CCA treatment. A comparable study of factory workers making CCA-treated foundations produced similar results.

The main reason why CCA-treated wood is considered safe is because the chemical is bound up within the cell structure of the wood and won't be released into the air or on the skin upon contact. Even if sawdust enters the lungs, CCA will not leach out of the wood particles into surrounding tissues. And according to the EPA, CCA-treated wood is acceptable for interior applications such as the walls of log homes, although not for cutting boards or countertops.

In spite of these assurances, common sense dictates that certain precautions be taken when working with CCA-treated lumber. Don't cut or sand the stuff inside, and wear goggles and a dust mask. Gloves are also a good idea, especially when handling wet lumber right off the pile— sometimes a liquid residue of the treatment chemical is present that hasn't been fully absorbed into the wood. Wash your hands after working with CCA-treated lumber, and wash your clothes separately from the rest of your household laundry.

One very real danger of CCA-treated wood is the formation of toxic gases and ashes by combustion. Never burn CCA-treated scraps or sawdust in stoves, fireplaces, or even in the open air. Instead, dispose of the waste at a landfill or by regular trash collection.

When working with lumber or railroad ties that have been treated with either penta or creosote, observe even stricter precautions than you would when using CCA-treated lumber. Always wear heavy clothing and gloves, and use a rubber respirator instead of a dust mask for maximum lung protection.

paid for, buy PT lumber that bears the label of a reputable treatment plant. Some companies, such as Osmose, have a national reputation that you can depend on.

Certain woods accept CCA treatment better than others. In the eastern United States, almost all CCA-treated lumber is southern yellow pine. In the west, Douglas fir is pressure treated as well. These woods have a hard, stringy texture that makes them difficult to work with hand tools. Although CCA-treated wood is paintable, the stringiness of the species used prevents the material from holding a finish as well as some of the finer-grained softwoods mentioned earlier. The high moisture content of most PT lumber also affects paintability and workability. Unless it's been kiln dried after treatment, PT lumber should be seasoned on site (see p. 22). PT lumber that has been dried after treatment will bear the letters "KDAT" on the grade stamp or label.

Before using any PT wood or wood preservatives, you should obtain the appropriate EPA Consumer Information Sheet from your supplier. The sheet contains specific information on the use, handling, and disposal of these products (see sidebar on the facing page).

Composites As forest products technology has advanced, man-made materials for outdoor use have appeared. Some of them, such as plywood, come in sizes that are not readily available in solid lumber. Others, such as wood-polymer lumber, offer superior durability in an outdoors environment.

Plywood—one of the first man-made wood products—consists of multiple wood veneers laminated together to form a sheet. Its great advantage lies in its ability to cover large areas quickly. By comparison, covering a surface with individual boards is time consuming. Plywood's weakness lies in its laminated edge, which is unsightly and doesn't hold fasteners well. Plywood also has trouble staying flat on its own, especially when wet. It will sag and warp unless supported by a framework of some kind. For these reasons, plywood is best used either as a skin to cover a frame (such as the siding of a garden shed) or as a panel that fits inside a frame (such as a flat-panel gate).

Plywoods for outdoor use can be divided into two categories: PT construction-grade plywood and marine plywood. PT construction-grade plywood is a rough product suitable for ground-contact applications such as foundations. It's available in the same species as PT woods. Sheet thicknesses of ½ in. and ¾ in. are readily available in the standard 4x8 size.

Marine plywood is a very high grade of exterior plywood made specifically for boat building. It is not pressure treated, but most of the species used, such as mahogany and teak, have natural decay resistance. It is also assumed that a finish will be applied and regularly maintained to provide protection from the elements. Marine plywood can be used in the garden for above-grade applications. Its high cost ($100 per sheet and up) may be justified for high-end projects, where premium species of solid lumber are used as well. Marine plywood is sold in a much wider variety of sizes than PT plywood. Thickness ranges from ⅛ in. through 1 in., and sheet sizes of 4x10, 4x12, and 4x16 are available in addition to the standard 4x8.

As the supply of large, old-growth trees has dwindled, manufacturers have looked for ways to make heavy

Wood-polymer lumber creates a durable, defect-free deck surface. (Photo courtesy of Trex.)

The wide, unbroken span of this pergola is carried by main beams of parallel-strand lumber. The lighter boards between the main beams are solid wood. (Designer/builder: Sam Cliffton.)

beams from smaller logs. The result is engineered lumber, an umbrella term for various types of man-made wooden beams.

One type of engineered lumber is the glulam beam (short for glue-laminated). It's essentially a stack of small boards glued face to face to make one large beam. In spite of its composite makeup, the glulam may be as strong as naturally grown timber of the same size. In fact, glulams often carry a higher strength rating than natural timbers of the same size because the boards used inside a glulam are inspected before manufacturing. The inspection prevents a glulam from having the kinds of severe knots or splits that are sometimes hidden inside natural timbers.

Glulams for exposed outdoor use are laminated with waterproof glue and pressure treated against decay. Curved glulams can be custom laminated on special curved forms. The combination of graceful shapes with high strength makes curved glulams good for garden bridges as well as for large pergolas.

A newer type of engineered lumber is parallel-strand lumber (PSL). PSL is composed of long, thin strands of wood bonded together under high pressure. PSL actually accepts pressure treatment better than solid lumber because it is more porous. You can see this if you compare the cut ends of a regular PT yellow pine 4x4 and a treated PSL 4x4. In the regular 4x4, the green color gives way to yellow toward the center, indicating that CCA retention diminishes away from the surface. The PSL 4x4 shows uniform retention throughout. The sole manufacturer of PSL at present is Trus Joist MacMillan, which sells both a treated and a nontreated product under the brand name Parallam (see Resources on p. 166).

When specifying the size of any engineered lumber beam, remember that these products do not necessarily have as much strength as a solid wood beam of the same dimensions. Also, their strength varies, depending on whether they're used above grade or below. When in doubt, consult the manufacturer, an architect, or an engineer.

Another important advance for outdoor woodworking has been the development of wood–polymer lumber. These synthetic products are made from recycled wood and plastic. The result is a material with most of the strength of wood and most (if not all) of the decay resistance of plastic. (At this writing, the leading manufacturer of wood–polymer lumber is Trex. See Resources on p. 166.)

Wood–polymer lumber can be cut and drilled with ordinary woodworking tools. It has no grain, so there's less splitting when a board is nailed close to its end. On the downside, the lack of grain makes for a rather drab, industrial appearance that may not fit in with natural surroundings.

At present, wood–polymer lumber is produced primarily as boards to be used for decking and seating (see the right photo on the facing page). Because it deflects, or bends, more than natural lumber, wood–polymer lumber is not currently recommended for structural framing members such as posts and beams.

Timbers for landscaping There are many types of naturally grown landscaping timbers suitable for the outdoors. Most lumberyards carry PT timbers in sizes like 4x4 and 6x6. Standard lengths range from 8 ft. to 16 ft. in 2–ft. increments, but lengths up to 26 ft. may be available by special order. Yards specializing in treated lumber sometimes stock 4x6s and 8x8s as well. Most PT timbers are planed at the mill, but sometimes they're available roughsawn. The roughsawn texture hides defects, such as knots and checks, and is really more appropriate for garden structures because of its rustic appearance. Another advantage of roughsawn timbers is that they run thicker than planed

timbers of the same nominal size. For instance, a planed 6x6 will measure 5½ in. by 5½ in. after planing, while a rough 6x6 will actually measure about 6 in. by 6 in. The same is true of smaller lumber sizes, such as 2x4s. However, the smaller sizes are almost always planed before sale, except at sawmills.

PT poles are cheaper than square timbers of the same approximate size. Their round, somewhat irregular shape gives them an organic feel that is appropriate in the garden. But their roundness also makes them more difficult to join together than square timbers. As a compromise, you can get semiround landscape timbers that are round on two opposing sides and flat on the other two sides (see the photo on p. 28). Having a flat top and bottom makes landscape timbers easy to stack and overlap.

Railroad ties that have been salvaged from railroad repair work are an inexpensive alternative to PT timbers. Standard railroad ties measure 7 in. by 9 in. by 8½ ft., and the cost of one of these is less than half the cost of an 8–ft.

An edging of natural logs adds character to this vegetable plot.

PT 6x6, which is 6 in. shorter and only measures 5½ in. square.

Railroad ties are more difficult to work with than PT timbers, though, for several reasons. For one thing, they're usually cut from hardwoods such as oak rather than the softwoods used for PT timbers. That makes ties heavier and harder to cut and drill. Another problem with ties is that they are treated with creosote, which means extra safety precautions (see p. 28). Creosote also has a tendency to accumulate on sawblades and drill bits, which causes them to heat up and cut poorly. On the upside, ties have a dark, funky appearance that can blend into a landscape better than PT timbers. Ties work particularly well for steps because their 7-in. thickness makes for a comfortable riser height.

The quality of salvaged railroad ties varies widely. Be sure to inspect the product at your lumberyard before purchasing or placing an order. A tie that is soft and crumbly is at the end of its useful life.

Logs cut from decay-resistant species such as cedar and locust can be used directly in the garden without being squared off (see the photo on p. 31). Indeed, the natural appearance of a log is desirable, although its roundness makes joinery a challenge. The bark of a log also adds to its rustic appearance. Unfortunately, bark tends to slough off after just a few seasons, especially when the log is placed directly on the ground. If you want the bark to stay on as long as possible, cut the tree down in winter, when its sap content is at a low point. Conversely, if you intend to peel the bark off the log before using it, fell the tree in summer, when the sap content is high. The sap running between the wood and the bark causes the bark to peel off more easily.

To peel bark, you can buy a specialized tool called a bark spud, which looks like an overgrown chisel. As an alternative, you can hew the bark off with a hatchet or try shoveling it off with a garden spade. Leaving a log outside for a season or two allows nature to do much of the work, as bugs and microbes attack the sugar-laden tissues just below the bark.

OUTDOOR FASTENERS

One of the most important decisions you'll have to make about your project is what fasteners to use. You'll have to balance the need for strength against aesthetic concerns. For instance, a large bolt that might look right at home on a heavy timber project would spoil the looks of a lacy trellis—and be unnecessary to boot. Conversely, you wouldn't use light finish nails to join 4x4s together—they simply wouldn't hold. As you gain experience with different fasteners, you will develop an intuitive sense of what works and what doesn't.

Nails

Nails come in a bewildering array of sizes, finishes, and types. The size of nails is generally measured by the penny, an arcane unit of weight. To complicate matters further, penny is abbreviated as "d" after a Roman coin called a *denarius*. Most lumberyards have a chart on the wall to help you translate the length of a nail into pennyweight (see the drawing on the facing page). The length of a nail should be at least twice the thickness of the piece being fastened, although three times the thickness is ideal.

Most nails are made of mild steel. For outdoor work, steel nails are galvanized,

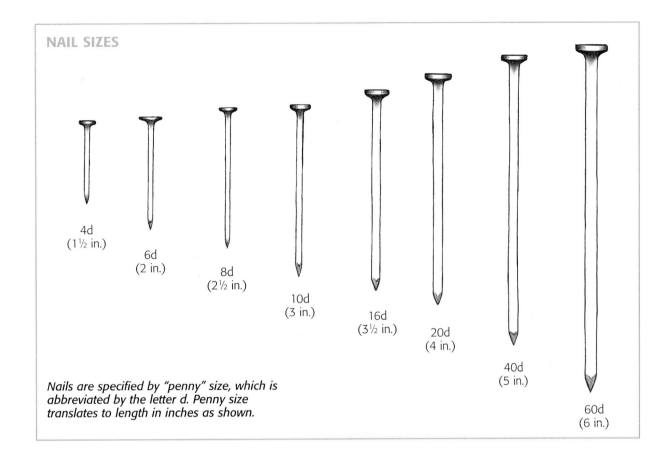

NAIL SIZES

4d
(1½ in.)

6d
(2 in.)

8d
(2½ in.)

10d
(3 in.)

16d
(3½ in.)

20d
(4 in.)

40d
(5 in.)

60d
(6 in.)

Nails are specified by "penny" size, which is abbreviated by the letter d. Penny size translates to length in inches as shown.

meaning that they are coated with a layer of noncorroding zinc. Steel nails that have not been galvanized are referred to as "bright." They should not be used outdoors. As a substitute for galvanized nails, stainless-steel nails are available in many shapes and sizes. Because they are noncorroding through-and-through, these nails are ideal for outdoor use. Their use also eliminates the stains sometimes caused by galvanized nails. The only drawback of stainless-steel nails is their high cost.

Nails can be divided into four broad categories: spikes, common nails, finish nails, and special-purpose nails (see the top drawing on p. 34). Spikes range from 6 in. to 12 in. in length. They're used to fasten heavy timbers together. As a sub-

stitute for spikes, you can use lengths of concrete reinforcing bar (called rebar) to fasten timbers together (see the sidebar in chapter 6).

Common nails run from 1½ in. to 6 in. long (4d to 60d). They are fairly stout in relation to their length, making them easy to drive. Galvanized common nails are good all-purpose fasteners for outdoor carpentry.

Finish nails have a very small head, which makes for a neat appearance. Galvanized finish nails can be driven flush with the surface, or they can be punched below the surface. The hole can then be filled with caulk or glazing compound prior to painting. Finish nails bend more easily than common nails because they are skinnier. Bending

NAILS FOR OUTDOORS

Spike   Common nail   Finish nail   Siding nail   Deck nail

Nails come in many styles. Spikes are for fastening heavy timbers. Common nails are good all-around fasteners. Finish nails have the neatest appearance. Siding nails and deck nails (special-purpose nails) have a spiral twist for greater holding power. All types should be galvanized for outdoor use.

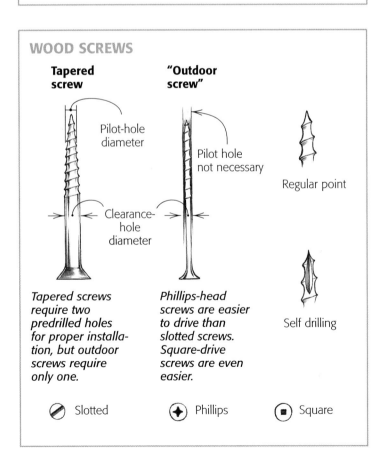

WOOD SCREWS

Tapered screw

Pilot-hole diameter

Clearance-hole diameter

"Outdoor screw"

Pilot hole not necessary

Regular point

Self drilling

Tapered screws require two predrilled holes for proper installation, but outdoor screws require only one.

Phillips-head screws are easier to drive than slotted screws. Square-drive screws are even easier.

Slotted   Phillips   Square

doesn't occur much in soft, even-grained woods such as cedar or redwood, but in a hard, stringy wood such as PT yellow pine, finish nails are difficult to drive. Another problem is that the small head of a finish nail cannot restrain unstable types of wood from warping. As the board warps, it simply slips past the finish nail's tiny head.

Special-purpose nails are available for particular applications. One type, called a deck nail, is designed specifically for installing PT decking. It's heavier than a finish nail, with a larger head, but not so beefy as a common nail. This combination makes it easy to drive yet discreet in appearance. Deck nails also have a spiral twist, which provides greater holding power. Siding nails are similar to deck nails but slightly skinnier.

Screws

The development of powerful cordless drills in recent years has made the use of screws more and more popular. Screws have two main advantages over nails: First, they have much greater holding power than nails. Second, screws can be easily removed, which makes fixing mistakes a lot easier.

Along with better screw-driving tools have come improvements in screws themselves (see the bottom drawing at left). Old-fashioned wood screws have a thick, tapering shank. These screws work fine, but they require that two different sizes of holes be drilled to avoid splitting the wood. First, a large-diameter clearance hole is drilled through the piece being fastened. Then, a smaller-diameter pilot hole is drilled in the piece being fastened to (the substrate). Old-fashioned tapered screws are available in plated steel, brass, or stainless steel. Plated screws rust quickly. Brass has good corrosion resistance, but because brass is a soft metal, it can be difficult to drive a brass screw without chewing up the drive recess. Stainless-steel screws offer maximum corrosion resistance and longevity. Unlike brass, they hold up well as they're being driven. For high-end projects, stainless-steel screws are worth the extra cost.

In recent years, the tapered screw has given way to a newer style generically referred to as outdoor screws. Outdoor screws are patterned after their indoor cousin, the black "drywall screw." Like drywall screws, outdoor screws have a straight, slender shank that can penetrate most substrates without a pilot hole. A clearance hole in the part being fastened is all that's necessary. In very soft wood, it's even possible to drive these screws through both pieces without drilling any hole whatsoever. One style of outdoor screw has a chisel point that drills its own hole as the screw is driven. These "self-drilling" screws are somewhat more expensive than regular pointed screws, but they save time.

Outdoor screws have one drawback when compared to old-fashioned tapered screws. Because outdoor screws are skinnier, they have less shear strength (the ability to withstand forces that are applied sideways to the screw's axis). In cases where heavy shear loads are to be applied, tapered screws may be preferable to the skinnier outdoor screws. For most garden projects, however, outdoor screws will work fine.

At one time, most screws had slotted heads, which are difficult to power drive because the tip of the driver bit tends to slip out of the slot. Nowadays, most screws have a Phillips head, which is easier to drive. A further improvement is the square-drive head. The square driver tip used to drive these screws almost

never slips out. Square-drive screws cost more than Phillips-head screws, but they can save a lot of frustration.

Before buying screws, inspect the drive recesses in their heads. In poorly galvanized screws, the drive recesses fill up with zinc, making the screws difficult to drive. To avoid this problem altogether, buy stainless-steel screws.

Lag bolts

Lag bolts are really overgrown screws (see the drawing above). They have a hex head that is driven by a wrench instead of a screwdriver for greater leverage. Lag bolts are available from ¼ in. to ¾ in. in diameter and up to 12 in. long. They do the same work as spikes, but they have much greater holding power. It's always necessary to drill a clearance hole for a lag bolt. A pilot hole isn't essential, but it eliminates the possibility of splitting the substrate.

Washers are used under a lag bolt's head to keep it from digging in during tightening. Washers also spread the pressure of the bolt head over a wide area. Otherwise, the wood under the

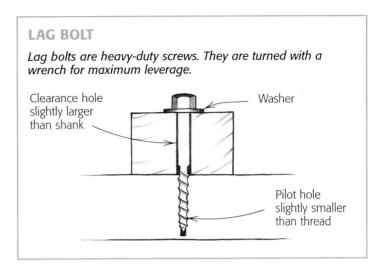

LAG BOLT

Lag bolts are heavy-duty screws. They are turned with a wrench for maximum leverage.

Clearance hole slightly larger than shank

Washer

Pilot hole slightly smaller than thread

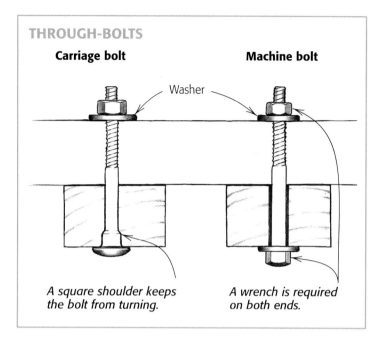

Carriage bolt

Machine bolt

Washer

A square shoulder keeps the bolt from turning.

A wrench is required on both ends.

until the washer under the nut just starts to crush into the wood surface. In soft, moist wood, the shoulder of a carriage bolt is apt to slip during tightening. In those cases it's better to use a machine bolt.

Framing connectors

Special-purpose framing connectors produce joints of great tenacity by applying the tremendous tensile strength of steel over a broad area around the joint (see the drawings on the facing page). In contrast, nails and screws "capture" only small amounts of wood under their heads. When a nail or screwed joint fails, it is often these small captured areas close to the end of a board that give way—not the fasteners themselves.

Unfortunately, most framing hardware has an industrial appearance that is ill-suited to garden architecture. One way to amend this is to paint your framing connectors a dark color. Wait a year or so after installing them on your project before painting to allow the galvanized surface of the connectors to weather; new galvanized steel does not hold paint.

Adhesives

Outdoor adhesives come in the form of liquid glues or caulk-type construction adhesives. Construction adhesives are easy to apply and some are formulated to bond under less-than-ideal conditions, including wet or frozen wood. However, they aren't as strong as some of the liquid glues.

The best all-around outdoor glue is a liquid yellow glue formulated for exterior use that requires no mixing (the leading brand is Titebond II). This type of

head of the bolt will gradually be crushed, causing the joint to loosen over time.

Through-bolts

Through-bolts (see the drawings above) pass completely through both pieces being fastened and are tightened with a nut and washer (unlike lag bolts, which pass completely through one piece but only partway into the other). One type of through-bolt, called a carriage bolt, has a round head with a square shoulder just below it. The corners of the shoulder bite into the surrounding wood to keep the bolt from turning while its nut is being tightened. Another type of bolt, called a machine bolt, has a hex head that is gripped with a second wrench while the nut is being tightened.

Carriage bolts work well in seasoned wood because the wood is hard enough to resist the turning action of the bolt's shoulder. The nut should be tightened

Steel framing connectors are easy to use and produce joints of great strength.

Post cap

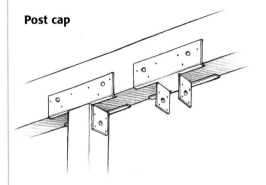

Connects a vertical post to a horizontal beam.

Top-flange hanger

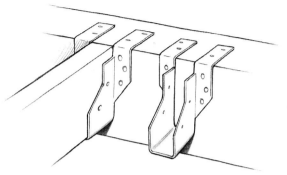

Ties horizontal beams together at a right angle (90°). Top flange affords maximum strength.

Skewable angle

Ties beams together at angles other than 90°. The connector can be bent to conform to the desired angle.

Face-mount hanger

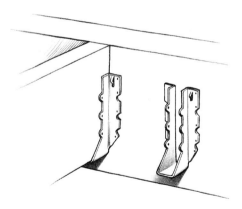

Also ties beams together at 90°. Not as strong as top flange hanger.

Plate strap

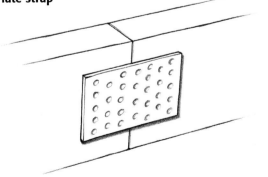

Ties beams together end to end.

glue can stand up to rain, sleet, and snow, but it can't be used underwater.

Two-part glues that require mixing are also used outdoors. Epoxies are two-part glues that are often sold in syringes that automatically dispense the correct amounts of each part. They set up very quickly, as fast as five minutes, and don't require much clamping pressure. Another two-part glue, resorcinol, offers the highest water resistance of all. It can be submerged underwater indefinitely without losing its grip. Resorcinol comes as a liquid, with a powdered catalyst that acts as a hardener. Polyurethane glues are a recent development. They are strong and waterproof but are rather expensive. Polyurethane glues work especially well with wet, unseasoned wood because the glue is actually activated by water. Other types of glue become diluted on wet wood, reducing their holding power.

OUTDOOR FINISHES

Finishes can change the appearance of your project. They can also inhibit deterioration by keeping out water and ultraviolet (UV) light. When choosing a finish, you must weigh these potential benefits against the long-term costs of maintaining a finish in good condition.

But before rushing at your project with a paintbrush, consider leaving it alone. Wood that has natural or man-made decay resistance can be left without a finish for a rustic, weathered appearance. Even not so decay-resistant species will last a long time without a finish, provided there is plenty of air circulation around them to keep moisture below the decay threshold. This option may be especially appealing if you are growing edibles on the structure and you would prefer not to grow your food near any chemically treated wood.

All exposed, unfinished wood eventually weathers to a silvery gray. It also undergoes other changes. The various kinds of warping, splitting, and checking described in the first part of this chapter are likely to occur, depending on the species. Another phenomenon that transpires is washboarding, or grain raising—an effect most easily seen on driftwood. If these "defects" aren't objectionable in the context of your project, don't burden yourself with a finish that will require regular maintenance.

Water repellents and preservatives

Water repellents are clear finishes that reduce some of the more drastic effects of weathering, such as warping and splitting, yet still allow wood to turn to its natural gray color. The principal ingredient in water repellents is wax, which is dissolved in an oil/solvent mixture that conveys the wax onto the wood surface. After water repellent has been applied, water will bead up on a wood surface as it does on a freshly waxed automobile (see the photo at left). After a few months, the beading action

A wax-based water repellent causes water to bead on this freshly coated surface.

dissipates, but the wood continues to absorb less water than it would without treatment. However, water-repellent finishes are short-lived in comparison to other finishes. Depending on the degree of exposure, they must be renewed every one to three years to remain effective.

In addition to wax, most water repellents contain a fungicide, which boosts decay resistance and controls mildew. This type of finish is known as a water-repellent preservative. Although it can prolong the life of above-ground wood if maintained regularly, it offers nowhere near the effectiveness of pressure treatment. Applying water-repellent preserv-

atives to below-grade wood, such as fence posts, is a waste of time.

Most water repellents can be painted over. The water repellent acts as a primer, reducing the amount of paint that is initially absorbed into the wood. Because water repellents are easy to apply, they are often used as a temporary finish to protect new work from the immediate harsh effects of rain and sun. The water repellent gives interim protection until paint can be applied. Before painting over a water repellent, however, check the label. Some water repellents contain so much wax that paint will not adhere properly to them.

A penetrating stain gives color to this poolside fence. Without a finish, the wood would quickly bleach to a silvery gray.

Varnishes

Varnish is a clear finish that forms a surface film rather than penetrate into the wood like water repellent. Varnish is mainly used on smooth wood to accentuate color and grain.

The best varnish for exterior use is marine spar varnish, which is formulated to have a high degree of elasticity to help it withstand extremes of temperature and moisture. Unfortunately, even marine spar varnish offers only short-lived protection. Varnishes exposed to sunlight usually crack and start peeling within two years, and the old varnish must be completely sanded off before refinishing. Varnishes also offer little protection against UV degradation because they contain no pigments. The only exterior projects that are suitable for a varnish are those that are at least partially shaded by some sort of overhang.

Semitransparent penetrating stains

Penetrating stains are similar to water repellents, except that they contain pigments. Pigments reduce the penetration of UV light, thereby protecting the wood as well as prolonging the life of the finish itself. Penetrating stains should only be applied over new wood or previous coats of water repellent or penetrating stain. Previous coats of paint or heavy-bodied stain will block the absorption of penetrating stain into the surface.

Penetrating stains are effective for a natural look. Pigment helps to obscure more prominent defects, such as knots and checks, but lets some of the wood grain show through. Penetrating stains do a particularly good job of hiding defects on roughsawn surfaces because a coarse-textured surface drinks up more finish than a smooth-planed surface does. Increased absorption also makes the finish last longer. Penetrating stains can last as long as eight years on rough-sawn surfaces, whereas four years is about the limit on smooth-planed work.

One of the biggest advantages of penetrating stains is that they do not crack or peel like film-forming finishes (such as varnishes) do. That means no more scraping in preparation for recoating. To prepare for restaining, the wood needs to be brushed clean with a wire brush, then hosed off.

Solid-color stains

Although called stain, this product is essentially a thin, flat paint. Most of these stains are latex or acrylic based and are formulated somewhat thinner than regular paints so that more surface texture will show through the finish. Like paint, solid-color stains (also called opaque stains) form a surface film that will eventually peel. Because solid-color stains contain less pigment than paint, their life is proportionally reduced. While paint systems are expected to last 7 to 10 years, solid-color stains last only 3 to 7 years. One advantage of solid-color stains is that they can be applied over previous film-forming finishes. They can also be applied over old penetrating finishes, as long as the surface is sanded first to remove surface oils.

Paints

No surface treatment can alter a project as dramatically as a coat of paint. White paint is the tried-and-true favorite for setting off an arbor or fence against a landscape. Colors are effective at relating structures to nearby architecture (see the photo at right).

Practically speaking, paint finishes provide the best protection against UV light because of their high concentration of pigments. (Dark colors offer more protection than lighter colors.) Paints also block the absorption of water better than other finishes, but this is a two-edged sword. Once moisture *does* penetrate a painted surface, the paint tends to hold that moisture inside, which can cause premature decay, especially of end grain. For that reason, surfaces that are exposed to standing water for long periods of time, such as decks, are better treated with a "breathable" finish such as water repellent or penetrating stain.

Oil-based paint contains pigment, an organic oil or resin, and a large quantity of a solvent, such as mineral spirits. As air-pollution controls have become more stringent, oil-based paints have become either more expensive or unavailable in some areas. And they are not convenient to use because brushes must be cleaned in solvent.

Latex paints contain pigments mixed with latex-based resins, as well as smaller quantities of organic solvents. Their primary solvent is water, which reduces air pollution, makes latex paints less toxic, and means brushes can be cleaned with soap and water.

As a wood surface dries and swells, or heats up and cools down, the paint film is subjected to a great deal of stress. So paint with good elasticity works the best. Although oil-based paints are prized for their sealing ability, they are not as elastic as latex paints. Latex paints stretch well and even have the ability to span over minor cracks in the wood surface or in the primer coat. Based on these pros and cons, a good plan for

This gate is visually tied to the house behind it by the color of its paint.

exterior paint is one coat of oil-based primer followed by two latex-based top coats. As technology improves, oil-based paints will probably fade from the scene altogether.

When shopping for paint, look at the solids content listed on the label. Solids are the only part of the paint that remain on the surface permanently; the solvents used to deliver the solids will evaporate. A 50% solids paint that costs only 5% more than a 40% solids paint is a better buy. When comparing latex paints, look for an all-acrylic binder, which is superior to a vinyl binder.

4 Fundamentals of Building Outdoors

So you've got your working drawings and your building permit, and the lumber was dumped off in your driveway yesterday. You're ready to start building. But before the sawdust starts flying, it pays to study a few how–to basics that are common to many kinds of garden structures.

Different structures require different types of construction. Frame construction is a way of joining individual parts into a frame or skeleton. Frame construction stands apart from "log–cabin" building techniques, which simply stack horizontal timbers in a way that's similar to masonry. Two types of frame construction are pole construction and timber framing. Pole construction refers to lightweight structures that transfer their weight directly to the soil via posts or poles, with no intervening masonry foundation. Timber framing refers to structures framed with heavy timbers instead of lightweight "stick" lumber such as 2x4s.

Beyond the type of construction, you'll need to determine your structure's finish. A finish can protect the project from weather and contribute to its look.

FRAME CONSTRUCTION

For thousands of years, woodworkers relied on nothing more than carefully wrought joints to hold buildings and furniture together. Today, nails and screws make it possible to join wooden members together with much less trouble. Metal framing connectors produce joints that are as strong as the most sophisticated mortise–and–tenon joint. In some cases, metal fasteners can also add an interesting accent, such as iron bolts used in heavy timber construction.

However, despite the benefits of fasteners, joinery gives a more integrated look than metal fasteners alone (see the drawings on the facing page). A half–lap joint, for instance, will keep the faces of two adjoining members flush (in the same plane). If the members were overlapped and bolted, there would be a visual disruption at the joint, which might not be desirable. If the members were simply butted and nailed, the joint would be flush but not very strong.

To create the best frame construction, fasteners and joinery should be used together (see the bottom drawings on

p. 44). For instance, a cross member that was simply nailed to a post would fail as soon as the nails started to pull loose, while a cross member would have direct wood-to-wood support. The nails don't carry weight—they merely hold the cross member in place.

Butt joints

A butt joint is really not a joint at all. One piece of wood simply butts into another. The strength of a butt joint depends entirely on the fasteners used. The joint is usually reinforced with nails driven at an angle—a process called toe-nailing (see the top drawing on p. 44). The nails should penetrate at roughly a 45° angle, with half the length of the nail ending up in each member.

To make toenailing easier and to prevent splitting, you can drill pilot holes in the piece being attached. The diameter of the holes should be slightly smaller than the diameter of the nail for a snug fit.

To create a stronger butt joint, you can substitute screws for nails. A screw will go in better if the starting hole in the piece being attached is slightly bigger than the screw. You don't need friction between a screw and its clearance hole because the clamping action of the screw's head does all the work.

Glue is entirely ineffective for reinforcing butt joints because one of the mating surfaces will be an end-grain surface. The end grain is so porous that it will immediately soak up any glue that's applied to it. The joint will therefore be starved for glue, making it weak.

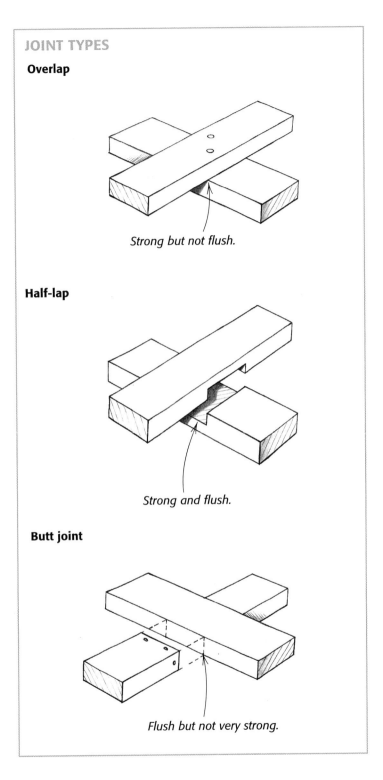

JOINT TYPES

Overlap

Strong but not flush.

Half-lap

Strong and flush.

Butt joint

Flush but not very strong.

FASTENING BUTT JOINTS

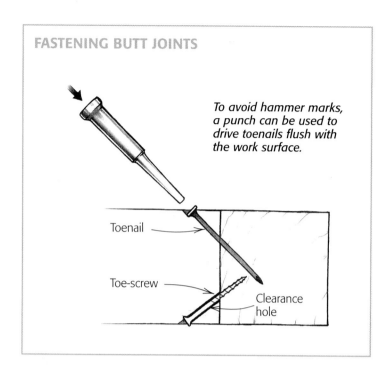

To avoid hammer marks, a punch can be used to drive toenails flush with the work surface.

Toenail

Toe-screw

Clearance hole

JOINTS AND FASTENERS WORKING TOGETHER

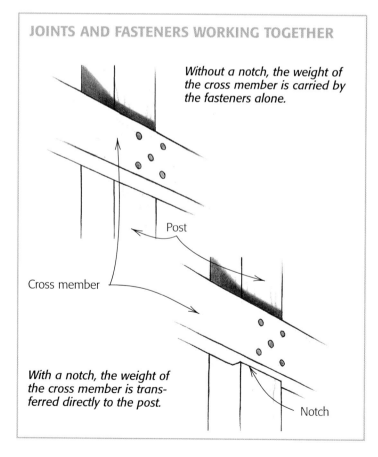

Without a notch, the weight of the cross member is carried by the fasteners alone.

Post

Cross member

With a notch, the weight of the cross member is transferred directly to the post.

Notch

Notching

Notching allows one piece to be partially "let in" to another (see the bottom photo on p. 46). It is especially effective for joining horizontal cross members, such as fence rails, to vertical posts (see the bottom drawing). By notching the post, a shoulder is created for the rail to sit on.

Notches in main structural members shouldn't be deeper than necessary or they will weaken the post. In the case of fence rails, a notch only ½ in. deep in a 4x4 post will provide plenty of bearing for the rail, without greatly weakening the post.

To cut a notch, begin by marking it on the piece with a pencil and a combination square (see the top left photo on p. 46). If similar notches are to be cut in other pieces, such as a set of four corner posts, you can line up all the pieces side-by-side and mark all the notches at once. After marking the faces of the notches on all four pieces, square down (draw perpendicular lines) on the sides of each piece to mark the shoulders. To mark the bottom of the notch, set your combination square to the depth of the notch and slide it along from one shoulder to the other, holding a pencil or a marker against the end of the square's blade.

Now make sawcuts at each shoulder down to the bottom of the notch. You can use a circular saw or a handsaw for this (for more on using a handsaw, see the sidebar on the facing page). If you're using a circular saw, you'll need to adjust the depth of cut. Make a few trial cuts in a test piece to make sure you have it right.

After cutting the shoulders of the notch, you'll need to remove the wood between the shoulders. Start with a series of crosscuts almost as deep as the

Cutting with a Handsaw

MAKING A SQUARE CUT

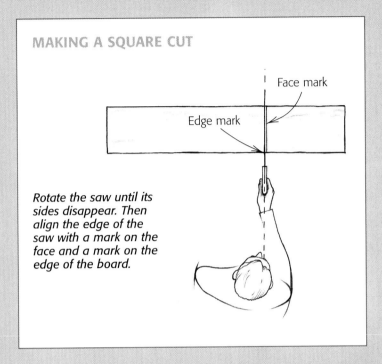

Face mark

Edge mark

Rotate the saw until its sides disappear. Then align the edge of the saw with a mark on the face and a mark on the edge of the board.

The trick to achieving a square edge with a handsaw is to get the saw started correctly. Position yourself so that you can see both the mark on the face of the workpiece and the mark on the edge. Move your head until these two marks appear as a straight line.

Now bring the blade of your handsaw up to the mark (see the drawing at left). Rotate the blade until its sides disappear and the top edge of the blade is all you see. Then adjust the saw sideways until it aligns with the combined face mark/edge mark on the work. Maintain a relaxed grip on the saw, with your forearm in line with the direction of the cut.

When starting the cut, place the thumb of your free hand against the blade to steady it (see the photo at left). Now draw the blade back toward you slowly. (If you try to push the blade at this point, it may skip around and cut your thumb!) A few gentle pull strokes will start a groove, or kerf, for the saw to ride in. Once a groove is established, you can begin sawing. Use long, easy strokes, and concentrate on keeping the blade, the face mark, and the edge mark all lined up.

Use your thumb to guide the saw when starting the cut. A few gentle pull strokes will establish a kerf for the blade to ride in.

You can use a combination square to scribe the bottom of a notch. The tool's handle can be locked anywhere along the ruler.

Remove the waste from a notch with a chisel. Make shallow crosscuts before chiseling so that the waste will break off easily.

Notches in this post help support the adjoining corner braces, taking most of the strain off the lag bolts used to secure the joints.

shoulder cuts. Take a chisel and split out most of the waste material (see the top right photo). The crosscuts allow most of the waste to come out easily in little pieces. You can try splitting the waste out in one big chunk, but if the grain of the wood wanders downward, you may end up splitting the wood deeper than you want to. (For more on using a chisel, see the sidebar on the facing page).

With the bulk of the material removed, pare the remaining wood down to the line with a chisel. Keep the flat side of the chisel down and work toward the center from the outside. Work at about a 45° angle to the direction of the grain, slicing off thin wafers of wood until you reach the bottom of the notch.

Lap joints

Lap joints are good, simple joints for garden carpentry (see the drawings on p. 48). Once you have mastered notches, lap joints will be almost as easy. A lap

Chisels and Planes

Chisels are used for chopping out waste wood and shaving flat surfaces. They can be pushed by hand (a technique called paring) or driven with a hammer or mallet. Plastic chisel handles can withstand the blows of a hammer, but wood-handled chisels should be beaten with a mallet to avoid damage.

Planes are essentially chisels held in a body that controls their cutting depth. The first plane bodies were wood, but longer-wearing iron bodies were developed in the 19th century. Iron planes were also easier to adjust.

The handiest plane for carpentry work is the block plane. It's a small plane designed to be used with one hand. To plane the edge of a board, plant one end of the board against something solid, and push the plane in the direction of the grain. If the plane iron, or blade, is sharp, one long, curled shaving will pirouette out

A block plane is used to shave the edge of a board.

of the tool. Experiment with the depth-of-cut adjusting screw to find the most effective setting.

To plane the face of a board, push the plane across the grain, producing thin wafers. The resulting surface will be rough but even—it can be sanded smooth. Planing the face of a board with the grain usually tears and digs into the surface.

joint is similar to a notched joint, except that both pieces are notched instead of one. When they overlap, the two pieces are flush.

To make a lap joint, notch one piece to a depth of half its thickness. Then lay it on top of the other piece, and use the notched piece as a template to mark the shoulders of the notch on the second piece. Nails, screws, or bolts can be used to hold the pieces together; glue

also greatly increases the strength of the joint.

When making a notch on the end of a piece, such as for a T half–lap joint, you can saw the waste material off in one piece rather than chiseling out the waste. To do this, saw the shoulder cut, then turn the piece on edge, and start the lengthwise cut. Hold the saw at a 45° angle so you can eyeball the cutline on the end of the stock as well as on the edge. If you have a vise at your disposal,

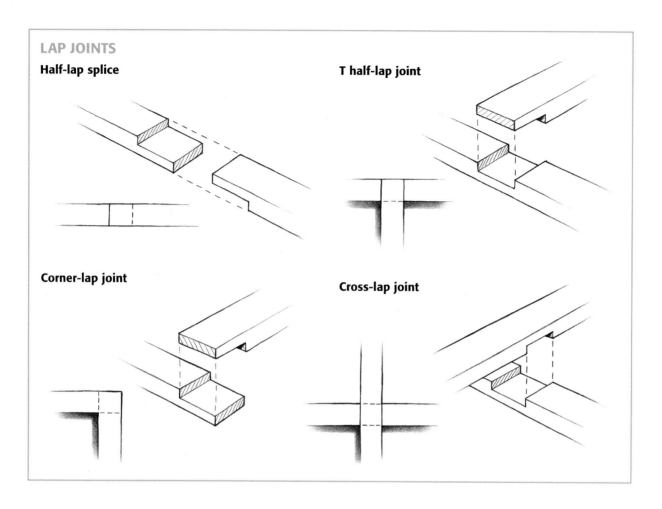

LAP JOINTS

Half-lap splice

T half-lap joint

Corner-lap joint

Cross-lap joint

When cutting a lap joint (like this half lap) with a handsaw, use a vise to hold the workpiece steady and at an angle.

clamp the workpiece at an angle to gain a more comfortable stance (see the photo at left). After you have sawn the lengthwise cut about halfway through, flip the piece around and saw in from the opposite edge as well. Keep cutting down until you reach the shoulder cut and the waste drops off.

Miter joints

Two tapering ends joined together create a miter joint. Most miter joints are cut at a 45° angle to produce a square corner. They are used a lot indoors for appear-ance's sake because they hide the rough

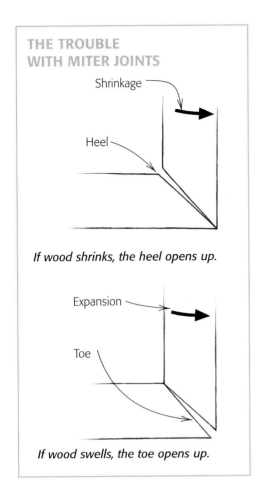

THE TROUBLE WITH MITER JOINTS

Shrinkage

Heel

If wood shrinks, the heel opens up.

Expansion

Toe

If wood swells, the toe opens up.

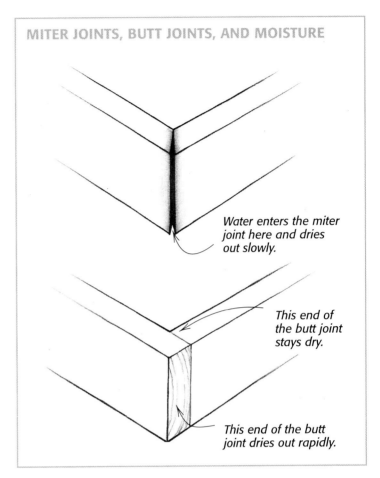

MITER JOINTS, BUTT JOINTS, AND MOISTURE

Water enters the miter joint here and dries out slowly.

This end of the butt joint stays dry.

This end of the butt joint dries out rapidly.

end-grain surface of a board. Unfortunately, miter joints don't work very well in outdoor carpentry for two reasons (see the left drawings above).

First, outdoor miter joints invariably open up due to wide fluctuations in dampness. Under hot, dry conditions, cross-grain shrinkage will cause the miter to open up at the heel—the inside corner of the cut. Under wet conditions, the wood swells in width, causing the joint to open up at the toe—the pointy end of the cut. The wider the boards, the more pronounced these gaps will be.

The second problem with miter joints is that, because of seasonal fluctuations,

water invariably enters the joint, where it's absorbed by the end grain. The end grain is mostly concealed and less air circulation reaches it, so the wood dries out slowly, leading to decay (see the right drawings above).

If a miter joint must be used, pin it together with nails or screws. This won't stop the shrinking and swelling, but it will at least hold the two pieces in alignment. Be sure to drill pilot holes. Not only will the holes prevent splitting, but they will also reduce the tendency of mitered pieces to slide against each other as they are fastened.

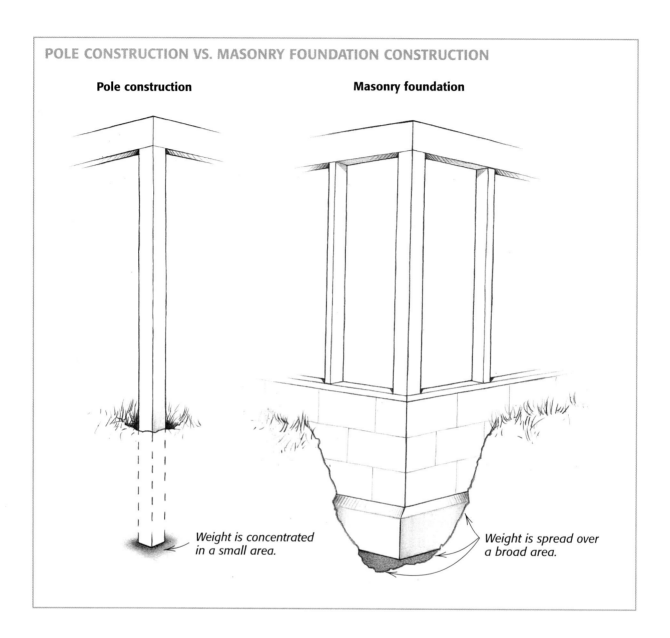

POLE CONSTRUCTION VS. MASONRY FOUNDATION CONSTRUCTION

Pole construction

Masonry foundation

Weight is concentrated in a small area.

Weight is spread over a broad area.

POLE CONSTRUCTION

Lightweight standing structures such as arbors, pergolas, and fences are examples of pole construction. In pole construction, the primary vertical members (square posts or round poles) bear directly on soil, without the benefit of a masonry foundation (see the drawings above). That means a pole-type structure requires much less digging than a conventionally built structure such as a house. In addition, the cost of a masonry foundation is saved. Pole structures are limited in weight, however, because their mass is concentrated on a relatively small area of ground. Too much weight can cause a pole structure to settle, especially when built on soft, compressible soil. Pole construction is more than adequate for most garden structures, but if you have something monumental in mind, you should consult an architect or a structural engineer about the possible necessity of a masonry foundation.

Laying out a pole structure

A pole structure begins as a series of holes in the ground. Locating these holes is a two-step process. The first step is to establish the structure's essential building lines. The second step is to locate individual posts in relation to the these lines.

For a straight fence, there is only one building line to worry about—a straight line drawn between two stakes. If the fence changes direction, stakes will be needed at each turning point. But for a three-dimensional structure such as a pergola, the structure's footprint needs to be staked out. In most cases, the foot-

print will consist of a rectangle or a series of connected rectangles. Of course other, more ambitious shapes are also possible, including triangles, circles, and octagons.

Rectangular footprints need to be truly square (have all 90° corners). Taking pains to make things perfect at this early stage will pay dividends throughout the rest of the building process. When a structure is out of square, measurements become confusing, cuts don't line up right, and everything becomes more difficult.

If you have a sheet of plywood on hand, the easiest way to lay out a square footprint for a structure that measures 4 ft. by 8 ft. or less is to make a template for the entire structure. As long as you make your template square, your layout will be square as well. To make things simple, you can use plywood, hardboard (such as Masonite), or even gypsum board. These products are manufactured square in the first place, which will give you a head start. Lay the template on

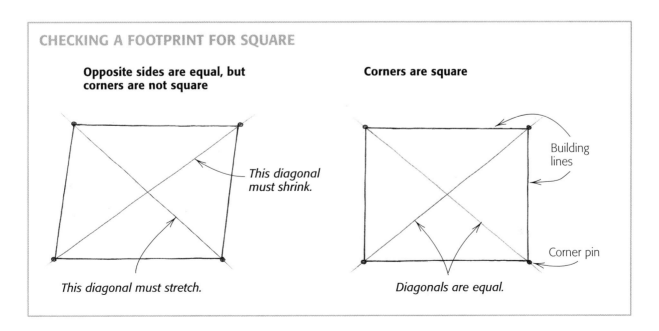

CHECKING A FOOTPRINT FOR SQUARE

Opposite sides are equal, but corners are not square

This diagonal must shrink.

This diagonal must stretch.

Corners are square

Building lines

Corner pin

Diagonals are equal.

An augur mounted on the back of a tractor can dig a large hole in a matter of seconds.

the ground and spray-paint around its edges. When you remove the sheet, a "shadow" will indicate the building lines. (Powdered lime can be sprinkled along the edges instead of spray painting.)

To lay out footprints that are larger than 4 ft. by 8 ft., you can use string. In the case of a rectangle, begin by driving four corner pins. (Wooden stakes can be used instead.) The distance between the pins must be equal on opposing sides of the rectangle, but a rectangle's diagonal measurements must also be equal for the rectangle to be square. If one diagonal is longer than the other, the layout must be shifted so that the long diagonal shrinks and the short diagonal stretches (see the drawings on p. 51). When the diagonals agree, your layout is correct.

Once the structure's footprint has been established, locate the actual post holes. First, make a cardboard template according to the post's dimensions (for instance, $3\frac{1}{2}$ in. by $3\frac{1}{2}$ in. for a 4x4 post). A scrap block of the same size lumber used for the post can be used instead of a template. Set the template (or block) into position, with its outside edges on the building line, then paint a circle around the template to indicate the hole itself (see the top photo at left). The diameter of the hole should be two to three times the width of the post, i.e., 8 in. to 12 in. for a 4x4. The same process must be repeated to locate posts between corners or when the footprint consists of multiple rectangles.

Digging post holes

Post holes can be dug mechanically or by hand, and their depth depends on a few variables (see the sidebar on p. 54). The easiest way is with a mechanical augur mounted on the back of a tractor (see the bottom photo on the facing page). The augur is raised and lowered hydraulically by a hitch on the back of the tractor, and the rotation of the augur is driven by the tractor's PTO (power takeoff). Two operators are required—one to work the tractor and another to position the augur. With such power and stability, large-diameter holes can be dug quickly, even in rocky soils. If you're contemplating a large project, ask around about tractors. Farmers, nurserymen, and fence contractors may have them for hire.

The next step down in hardware is a two-man powered augur (see the photo at right). This machine is raised and lowered by hand, while the rotation of the augur is driven by a gas engine. Operating a two-man powered augur is straightforward in homogenous soils but can be a test of will in rocky ground. When the leading edge of the augur strikes a rock, the considerable force of the machine bounces back at the operators. If you enjoy rototilling, you'll love earth auguring. And despite the bone-jarring operation and the noise and fumes of a gas engine, you can get a lot done in a day with one of these machines.

In addition to two-man augurs, there are one-man models available. In terms of balance, two persons are much better than one, but one-man augurs work well in fine, sandy soil.

If you don't want to use machinery of any type, and you want to build up your shoulder muscles, manual post-hole digging is for you. To start, outline the hole with a pointed shovel. If the sod is too thick to pierce with a shovel, a few whacks with a heavy mattock will cut through the surface roots. You can excavate the first 12 in. or so with a shovel, but beyond that point the sides

Digging with a two-man powered augur is faster than digging by hand.

of the hole will restrict the levering action of the shovel handle, so you'll need to switch to a post-hole digger, sometimes called a clam-shell digger. This tool has a pair of scooping blades attached to long wooden handles. To use it, plunge the digger down into the hole with the handles pressed together. Spread the handles to pinch a scoopful of earth between the blades, then remove the soil and set it to the side of the hole.

In hard soils, you'll have to loosen the earth between every few jabs of the post-hole digger, which is where bars come in. Bars are available in many variations, but the most popular style, called a digging bar, has a wide chisel point at one end and a disk-shaped head at the other end (see the drawing on p. 55). The head makes it easier to lift a smooth bar out of a hole with sweaty

Depth of Post Holes

It's difficult to make hard-and-fast rules about the depth of post holes because several factors come into play. Of primary concern is the height of the post above grade, or ground level; the taller the post, the deeper it needs to be sunk in the earth for it to be sturdy. For instance, a 3-ft.-high picket fence post would only need to go down about 1 ft., while an 8-ft.-high pergola post would require a hole at least 2 ft. deep.

Another variable affecting the depth of post holes is the material used for backfilling. Hard, dry soil resists movement better than soft, wet soil, so the harder the backfill, the shallower the hole can be. Concrete is the hardest backfill of all.

A post that's been set in concrete will be much sturdier than a similar post set in dirt.

To see how deep a post hole needs to be, it's best to experiment. Dig the first hole to a depth of about one quarter the overall length of the post. Set the post, backfill it, and see how it feels. If the post wiggles, pull it out and go deeper. If the post feels rock solid and you've been breaking your back, see if you can get away with a little less depth on the next one.

Unlike structural foundations, garden posts don't need to be set below the frost line (the depth below which the ground never freezes). Frost may lift garden posts slightly during the freeze-thaw cycle, but they will settle back down come spring. A few shovelfuls of gravel in the bottom of a hole can minimize frost heave by letting water drain away from the bottom of a post.

The best way to determine the appropriate depth of a post hole is to experiment. Dig the hole to about one-quarter the length of the post. Set the post and backfill. If the post moves, pull it out and dig deeper.

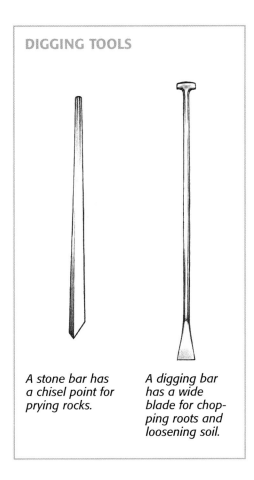

DIGGING TOOLS

A stone bar has a chisel point for prying rocks.

A digging bar has a wide blade for chopping roots and loosening soil.

hands and can also be used as a ram for driving rocks during backfilling.

The stone bar is a cousin of the digging bar with a narrow chisel point (see the left drawing above). The stone bar can fit between tightly packed rocks where the wider digging bar cannot reach.

The chisel edge of a bar can easily shear through small roots. Larger roots can be hacked through with the bar, chopped with an ax, or cut with a chainsaw. When using a chainsaw, carefully remove as much dirt from around the root as possible to avoid dulling the chain. Since it's difficult to get dirt out from under a root, don't cut all the way

through. Instead, bust through the last inch or so with an ax or bar.

Placing the posts

Once the holes are dug, it's time to put in the posts. If pressure-treated (PT) timbers are cut up for posts, be sure to put the uncut end of the timber down into the hole. This factory end is more decay resistant than the cut end. To avoid pieces with two cut ends, order appropriate lengths. In other words, for 4-ft. fence posts, order 8-ft. lengths rather than 12-ft. lengths, because a piece taken from the middle of a 12 footer would have no factory end.

Posts are most susceptible to decay at grade level, where both moisture and oxygen are abundant and where the greatest structural stresses on the post occur. For these reasons, when setting tapered cedar or locust poles, place the thicker end of the post in the hole to maximize the amount of wood where it's needed most.

Backfilling

Posts can be set in concrete or simply backfilled with rocks and soil. Concrete obviously costs more but will produce a stronger and more precise installation. Concrete works especially well in marshy places, where water stands in the post hole. In that case, dry concrete is poured around the post. The concrete then cures underwater. When wet concrete is called for, it can be mixed on site by hand or in a drum-type cement mixer. Concrete can also be purchased as redi-mix, which is concrete that's mixed in a truck on its way to the site. Whatever type of backfill you use, don't add it all at once; add some, then check

The amount of concrete backfill required to set a post depends on the size of the post and on the size of the hole. Let's take the example of a 4x4 post being set 2 ft. deep in an 8-in.-diameter hole. The volume of the hole is calculated as follows:

$$\pi r^2 \text{ (cross sectional area of hole) x}$$
$$\text{(depth of hole in inches)}$$
$$= \text{volume of hole,}$$

$$or,$$

$$3.14 \times 4^2 \times 24 = 1,205 \text{ cu. in.}$$

But part of that volume is taken up by the post, so you need to subtract from this figure the volume of the post below grade, which in this case would be 4 x 4 x 24, or 384 cu. in. The balance is the amount of concrete required, which in this case would be 821 cu. in. The easiest way to convert this number to cubic yards, which is how concrete is ordered, is to divide the balance by 36^3, or 46,656 (the number of cubic inches in a cubic yard). To determine the requirements for hand mixing concrete, see the chart on the facing page.

that the posts are plumb (straight up and down) before adding more.

Redi-mix concrete For jobs requiring 1 cu. yd. or more of concrete, the best way to backfill is to order redi–mix concrete. You will need an accurate idea of how much concrete is required when you place your order (see the sidebar above).

Before the redi–mix truck arrives, you should carefully consider the scenario for getting concrete from the truck to the post holes. If you're backfilling fence posts along a road, you can simply pour concrete into each hole directly from the truck's chute as the truck ambles along. More frequently, however, the concrete will need to be poured into wheelbarrows and then distributed to each hole as required. Have at least one extra helper and wheelbarrow in service for

small jobs and a larger crew on hand for quantities of several yards or more.

You'll need the extra help because concrete starts hardening as soon as a batch is mixed at the concrete plant, so the quicker it's poured, the less likelihood there will be of the concrete partially setting in the truck. Under no circumstances will a truck driver allow concrete to harden fully in his truck. If you don't get it poured in time, the driver will just pour it out, and you will be the proud owner of a big, gray blob.

To expedite the pour, provide easy access for wheelbarrows to each post hole. That means clearing away brush and other obstructions, as well as bridging difficult terrain with planks.

Hand-mixed concrete If the redi-mix scenario sounds a little nerve-racking, you can opt for mixing concrete your-

CONCRETE REQUIREMENTS

Hole diameter	8 in.	10 in.	12 in.
For 4-in. by 4-in. post			
12 in. deep	36 lb.	65 lb.	101 lb.
18 in. deep	54 lb.	98 lb.	152 lb.
24 in. deep	71 lb.	130 lb.	202 lb.
30 in. deep	89 lb.	163 lb.	253 lb.
For 4-in. round pole			
12 in. deep	39 lb.	69 lb.	105 lb.
18 in. deep	59 lb.	103 lb.	157 lb.
24 in. deep	79 lb.	137 lb.	209 lb.
30 in. deep	98 lb.	172 lb.	262 lb.
For 3-in. round pole			
12 in. deep	45 lb.	74 lb.	110 lb.
18 in. deep	67 lb.	112 lb.	166 lb.
24 in. deep	90 lb.	149 lb.	221 lb.
30 in. deep	112 lb.	186 lb.	276 lb.

To determine the quantity of bags, divide by lb./bag (typically 20 lb. or 80 lb.).

self. For small jobs, it's easiest to use a dry concrete premix that contains portland cement, sand, and gravel already mixed in the correct proportions—all you need to do is add water and stir. A bag of premix will typically produce ⅔ cu. ft. of concrete. (See the chart above for other premix requirements.)

For larger jobs, it's cheaper—by about 75%—to buy sand and gravel in bulk and mix them on site with portland cement. It also ensures that the mix will be fresh. The normal ratio is one part cement to two parts sand and four parts gravel. A sack of cement contains 1 cu. ft., or $\frac{1}{27}$ cu. yd., so a typical materials order for 1 cu. yd. of concrete would be 1 cu. yd. of gravel, ½ cu. yd. of sand, and seven sacks (about ¼ cu. yd.) of cement. The volume of concrete produced doesn't equal the combined volume of the ingredients because the sand and cement particles fit in between the gravel stones after mixing.

You'll need to wear eye protection when mixing because concrete is mildly caustic. Concrete can be hand mixed with a shovel or a hoe. It's best to mix

Concrete for setting posts should be mixed to a stiff consistency.

leave excessive moisture on the palm of your hand (see the photo at left). Rinse your hands after performing this test.

For jobs that are too small for ordering redi-mix but too big to mix by hand, you can rent a cement mixer. Premix can be poured directly into the mixer, while bulk ingredients are usually measured in by the shovelful. You will need a hitch on the back of your vehicle to tow the mixer from the rental yard. If you don't have one, most rental yards will fix you up with a hitch at minimal cost.

Soil To backfill a post hole with soil, begin by tossing a stone or two on each side of the post. Pound the stones down tightly around the base of the post. To push the post in one direction or the other, keep adding rocks on the opposite side and drive them in. The post can also be prodded by levering against the side of the hole with a digging bar or a 2x4. When the post is positioned properly in relation to the building line, add a few shovelfuls of soil. Pack the soil in and add some more rocks if you have them. Repeat until the hole is backfilled about halfway.

Check the post with a level to see if it is out of plumb and push it back to plumb if it is. Continue backfilling. Check the post with a level again when the hole is filled, and make any final adjustments by shoving the post and jamming in additional stones just below the surface. Whenever posts are set in a row, eyeball down the row from one end—any leaners will be easily detected from this vantage point.

on a flat surface such as a sheet of plywood so the ingredients have plenty of room to move around. Once it's mixed, shovel the concrete into a wheelbarrow for transport. Mixing directly in the wheelbarrow saves lifting, but the contours of the wheelbarrow make mixing slower. If you have a helper, another effective way to mix concrete is to bounce the ingredients up and down on a plastic tarp like a trampoline.

The amount of water added to a batch of concrete depends on the dampness of the sand used. If the sand pile is soaked after a rain, no additional water may be necessary. But premix is packaged bone dry, so a fair amount of water must be added. Rather than measure the amount of water, keep an eye on the consistency of the mix. When you pick up a handful and squeeze it, the concrete should keep its shape but not

A jumbo circular saw can cut a 6x6 in a single pass.

You can use a chainsaw to clean up the bottom of a notch by sweeping the cutting bar from side to side.

TIMBER FRAMING

Heavy timbers are best known for earth-retaining projects such as walls and raised beds, but they can also be used for standing structures such as pergolas and bridges when a large scale is called for. This branch of frame construction is known as timber framing. While the structural principles used in timber framing are the same as for general carpentry, handling and working with heavy timbers requires some special tools and techniques (see the sidebar on p. 63).

The easiest way to cut heavy timbers is with a chainsaw (see the sidebar on p. 60). The chainsaw has a reputation as

A bow saw can cut large timbers quickly. Use a block of wood to line up the blade instead of your thumb.

Chainsaw Safety

Even small chainsaws are dangerous. Mishandling them can lead to injuries ranging from minor cuts to severe lacerations of the face, shoulder, and neck, sometimes causing amputation or death. All tools deserve respect, but when it comes to safety precautions, chainsaws are in a class by themselves.

Ear and eye protection are an absolute must when operating a chainsaw to avoid the noise and dust it spews out. Gas chainsaws also produce poisonous carbon monoxide, so never operate a gas chainsaw without ample ventilation. If you want to work, say, in the garage, use an electric chainsaw or a circular saw.

One of the unseen dangers of chainsaws is the phenomenon known as kickback. As the chain races around the bar, it carries with it terrific momentum. If the chain is forced to a sudden stop, a jerk or kick will be the result. This sudden stop can be caused by making accidental contact with an object or by being pinched when the workpiece being cut sags in the middle.

Which direction the saw jerks depends on where the chain meets sudden resistance. If resistance occurs on the bottom of the bar, the saw (and the operator) will be tugged toward the workpiece. If resistance occurs on the top of the bar, the saw will be shoved back toward the operator.

Another type of kickback called rotational kickback is even more dangerous. It occurs when the chain is suddenly stopped in the upper corner of the bar nose (see the drawing on the facing page). This type of kickback also occurs when the chain is stopped or pinched, but in this case, the bar may be thrown up and back toward the operator.

There are a number of ways to guard against kickback. Your first line of defense is to use a low-kickback chain. These safety chains are now standard equipment on homeowner-type saws. Second, don't use the more powerful logging-type chainsaws

When cutting with a chainsaw, keep your thumb curled under the handlebar and your elbows locked.

for carpentry, because the more powerful the saw, the more potent the kickback. Finally, maintain a correct grip and stance, so that the force of a kickback will be automatically resisted by your body. Always keep both hands on the saw. Keep your right hand on the throttle and your left hand on the handlebar, with your left thumb curled underneath the handlebar (see the photo on the facing page). Keep your left arm straight, locked at the elbow, and stand with your legs apart, knees flexed. Above all, stay alert—don't operate a chainsaw when you're tired or upset.

It's advisable to use a bar-nose guard on your chainsaw when doing carpentry work. The guard bolts to the end of the chainsaw bar, virtually eliminating rotational kickback. Bar-nose guards come as original equipment on some saws or can be purchased as an attachment from chainsaw dealers. When starting a chainsaw, keep your right foot inside the handle and your left hand on the handlebar.

One of the most important chainsaw safety rules is to keep the engine idle properly adjusted. When this adjustment is correct, the engine will continue running between cuts but at such a slow speed that the chain doesn't move. A chain that moves when it should be idling is a hazard.

ROTATIONAL KICKBACK

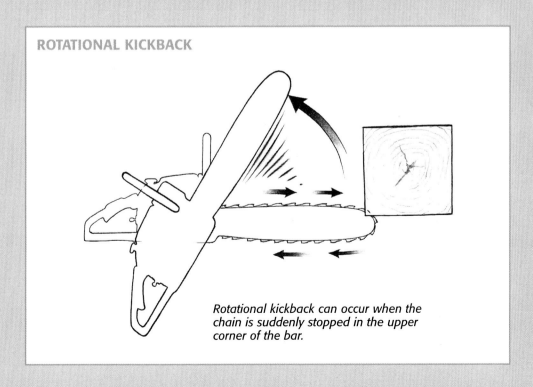

Rotational kickback can occur when the chain is suddenly stopped in the upper corner of the bar.

a rough-cutting monster, but with a little practice you can get surprisingly accurate results. The chain should be sharp and kept properly tensioned. If the chain hangs down more than $\frac{1}{8}$ in. below the bottom of the bar, tighten it up. Use a thick carpenter's pencil to lay out a cutline on both the top and side of your timber and line up the bar of a chainsaw much as you would with a handsaw.

Chainsaws also work well for rough notching. First, make the shoulder cuts and the crosscuts in the waste section. Knock out the bulk of the waste with a hammer. To clean up the bottom of the

A random-orbit sander speeds up a sanding job.

notch, sweep the chainsaw bar carefully from side to side (see the top right photo on p. 59).

To cut timbers more precisely, use a circular saw. A regular $7\frac{1}{4}$-in. circular saw only cuts about $2\frac{1}{2}$ in. deep, so to complete a crosscut you'll need to cut in from all four sides and then finish the cut with a handsaw. Jumbo circular saws are available that will cut through a 6x6 in a single pass (see the top left photo on p. 59). If you have a large project to build, such as a retaining wall, a jumbo saw will speed up your cutting considerably.

If you have only a few timbers to cut, try a bow saw. This type of handsaw is used mainly for tree pruning, but it works equally well on timbers. A word of caution: When starting a cut with a bow saw, be careful because the blade of the bow saw is tensioned, causing it to bounce around. Beginners should use a block of wood rather than their thumb to guide the first few strokes of the saw (see the bottom photo on p. 59).

FINISHING TECHNIQUES

Outdoor finishes are less finicky to apply than their indoor cousins. On the other hand, outdoor finishes need to be renewed much more frequently, so it pays to use the proper tools and techniques.

Careful preparation can make a potentially messy job go smoothly and will produce the best final product. Brushing is the best all-around method for applying finishes, but rolling can speed things up without much extra trouble. For large projects, or those with fussy surfaces such as lattice panels,

Moving Timbers Safely

Unseasoned timbers can be incredibly heavy, so it pays to be careful when moving them. First, to avoid back injury, lift with your knees bent and your back straight. You can alleviate back stress by dragging instead of carrying. Wrap a length of rope around a timber so that two people can carry one end while the other end drags behind. The weight lifted by each person is then only 25% of the timber's weight. But it's better to avoid lifting altogether, if possible, so have the timbers dumped off the truck close to the building site. You can also slide timbers along the ground by using small-diameter logs or pipes as rollers.

Overhead lifting is more difficult than simply moving the timbers. To raise a medium-size timber onto posts, begin by bracing the posts securely in both directions. Then set up a sturdy scaffold consisting of sawhorses and heavy planks high enough that a person standing on it will have the tops of the posts about chest high. Lift or slide the timber up on the scaffold, then climb up on the scaffold, and position yourself and your helpers at one end of the timber. First lift one end of the timber onto its post, and hold it in place with scab blocks (short blocks that temporarily straddle the top of the post). Then lift the other end onto its support (see the top photo at left).

Another way to raise a heavy beam is to use skid poles (see the bottom photo at left). These can be square timbers or round poles, but poles actually work better because there will be less contact area (and friction) as a timber slides up the pole. Depending on the height of the lift, timbers can be pushed up the skid poles, pulled with ropes, or both. Pulling with a truck or tractor is also possible.

For large projects, heavy equipment will lift timbers quickly and safely. A backhoe can set beams as high as 12 ft. off the ground, and a small crane, sometimes called a cherry picker, can go even higher.

After lifting one end of the post into place and securing it with scab blocks, set the other end in place.

You can slide a heavy timber into place by pushing it up a pair of skid poles. A board is used here for pushing.

spraying can save an enormous amount of time. Dipping works particularly well with thinned-down products such as stain or water repellent, which are difficult to apply with a brush.

Preparing the surface

Applying a finish can seem anticlimactic after the excitement of seeing your project take shape, so you may be tempted to slap on a coat of paint and call it a day. But patience and careful preparation are necessary at this stage to produce a finish that is functional, attractive, and durable. Surfaces that will come in contact with human bodies, such as benches, should be sanded to avoid splinters. Sanding also keeps a paint film from cracking at the corners. Start with 50-grit paper and finish up with 80 grit. Round all corners and edges slightly.

If you have a lot of area to sand, an electric sander will speed things up. The random-orbit type is a good all-around sander that is quick cutting and maneuverable (see the photo on p. 62). Belt sanders cut quicker than random-orbit sanders, but they are clumsier and don't reach into tight spaces as well. Orbital pad sanders are slower than random-orbit sanders. They're used mainly for fine furniture and cabinetry.

To protect surrounding surfaces and plantings during finishing, spread drop cloths. Canvas drop cloths are preferable to plastic, because they absorb drips and are limp enough to conform to irregular surfaces.

Read the label on the can of finish thoroughly to find information on things like proper temperature and compatibility with previous finishes. Stir the contents until all solids are dissolved; stirring takes a long time with stains, which don't dissolve as readily as paint solids. To speed up the process, you can use a paint paddle inserted in an electric drill. The solids in stains and water repellents tend to settle out quickly, so these finishes should be stirred frequently during use.

Brushing

For small- to medium-size projects, brushing remains the simplest and most effective way to apply a finish. Just about all outdoor finishes can be applied with synthetic-bristle brushes (nylon or polyester). For a high-gloss varnish finish, a natural hog-bristle brush will leave fewer brush marks, but the difference is minor. Natural-bristle brushes can also be used for all oil-based finishes but not for water-based finishes—natural bristles absorb water, causing them to go limp.

A 3-in. and a 4-in. brush will cover most of your outdoor finishing needs. Since absolute smoothness of finish isn't required in the garden, you won't need a top-of-the-line $15 brush. On the other hand, steer clear of bargain-basement brushes. Not only do they produce poor surface quality, but they also don't hold finish well. As a result, the finish runs all over the place.

For small projects, disposable foam brushes save on cleanup time. These brushes work remarkably well on smooth to semismooth surfaces. They don't work well on rough surfaces, though, because the foam is easily torn.

Begin brushing at the top of your project and work down, brushing out drips and runs as you go. Hold the

brush at a slight downward angle when–
ever possible to keep the finish flowing
off the tip, rather than flowing back
toward the heel of the brush.·

The most demanding brushwork is
required by high–gloss enamels. A poor
enamel finish will show runs, sags, and
coarse brush marks. These flaws don't
occur as much when painting a hori–
zontal surface, because gravity causes
the enamel to flow out evenly in all
directions. For that reason, it's good to
enamel small projects or individual
parts in a flat position before they're
installed, turning them in phases to dry.
The quality of the finish will justify the
extra time it takes.

If enameling a vertical surface is
unavoidable, keep your brush as dry as
possible, working the paint around
aggressively. After spreading a thin, even
coat over the entire surface, brush it out
across the grain. Finally, give the surface
a feather–light brushing with the grain.
Inspect the surface from different angles
to make sure you haven't missed any
spots. Inspect the surface again after
15 minutes and brush out any sags that
have occurred. If possible, prop a clean
sheet of plywood over the work as a
temporary roof to protect the finish
from airborne debris while it dries.

Rolling

Rolling is an easy way to speed up a
large finishing project such as a pergola.
A narrow 4–in. roller works well, and
the length of the nap depends on the
roughness of the project's surface. Very
smooth finish boards require a short
nap; regular lumber, including pressure
treated, takes a medium–nap roller; and
rough–sawn lumber requires a long nap.

**Spray painting makes short work of outdoor
finishing projects. Move the gun parallel to
the work to apply an even coat.**

When rolling, use long, overlapping
strokes. If possible, roll boards in a hori–
zontal position before assembly; paints
will flow out better, and stains will have
a more even distribution of pigment. If
you must work on vertical boards and
you need to extend your reach, you can
attach a pole handle to the roller.

Stains and water repellents are readi–
ly absorbed into a wood surface after
being rolled on. However, because paint
is somewhat thicker, it should be
worked around on the surface a little

An HVLP spray rig is compact and fairly inexpensive.

after rolling to get a good grip. Give it a few vigorous brush strokes right after applying the paint.

Spraying

Spraying is by far the quickest way to apply outdoor finishes (see the photo on p. 65). It's especially timesaving on finishing work with lots of nooks and crannies, such as lattice panels. Conventional spray equipment is expensive and tricky to use, but recent advances in spray technology have made spray finishing practical for the homeowner as well as for the professional.

Conventional spray rigs consist of a high-pressure air compressor, a hose, and a spray gun. The tip of the gun can be adjusted to produce different spray patterns, depending on the shape of the object being sprayed. A conventional sprayer driven by a gas engine is still the best choice for remote projects (such as pasture fences) where electricity is not available.

A new type of sprayer, generically referred to as an HVLP (high-volume low-pressure) sprayer, is the most practical for the do-it-yourselfer, because the equipment is less expensive and more compact (see the photo at left). Prices for an HVLP unit start at about $250, while the cost of a good conventional spray outfit starts at about $500.

A third type of sprayer, called an airless sprayer, is an electric unit that delivers a finish very quickly. This type of sprayer is good for large projects within reach of electricity. An airless sprayer starts at about $400. All three types of sprayers can be rented.

Most finishes can be sprayed. Thin finishes, such as water repellent and stain, can be sprayed as-is from the can. Heavier finishes, such as oil paints, will spray better if they're thinned down from their normal brushing consistency. However, there is a limit to how much some finishes, such as latex paint, can be thinned, so consult the label. (Some latex paints are not recommended for any spray application whatsoever.) For thick finishes that can be sprayed, guns have interchangeable tips with different-size spray orifices.

After thinning your finish, pour it into the cup of the spray gun through a funnel-shaped filter (available at paint stores). If solid particles enter the gun, they can clog the tip. To strain a heavy finish, you can make your own filter out of insect screen (see the photo on the facing page).

Because spraying produces a breathable mist, it is important to use lung protection. While dust masks are adequate for sanding dust, they don't provide sufficient protection against spray mist—for that you need a respirator with a charcoal filter. When you start smelling finish through the respirator, it's time to change the filter. It's also advisable to wear a stocking cap when spray painting, to keep finish out of your hair.

Before spraying your project, practice on a few test pieces. Good spray technique depends on maintaining a consistent distance between the spray tip and the workpiece. Start spraying to one side of the work, pass over the work in a straight, steady sweep, and release the trigger after you are beyond the work. If you make a U-turn over the work, you will leave extra material at the edge which is liable to run.

Dipping

Sometimes individual parts such as fence pickets can be dipped in water repellents or stain before assembly. Pour about a gallon of finish into a 5-gal. pail. Stick one end of the part into the bottom of the pail to give the end grain a good soak. Meanwhile, use a brush to draw some finish up onto those portions of the workpiece that aren't submerged. Turn the part around to dip the other end. Lift the part above the pail to drain for a few seconds, and then set it aside to dry. Dipping can be used for paints as well as for stains, but because paint is thicker, drips may harden as the work dries.

To keep the spray gun from clogging, strain the paint. Use a piece of insect screen as a filter and a milk jug as a funnel.

5 Borders and Steps

To garden is to arrange the landscape according to your tastes and necessities. But Mother Nature's concern for these matters is, shall we say, rather low. Plant species stage territorial invasions and counterattacks. Rain washes soil from one place to another. Gravity, that great leveler, joins in the onslaught, shoving your best-laid plans aside with slow, steady purpose.

Wood is one of the most effective weapons in this trench warfare of the garden. In its simplest application, borders can be laid on level ground to define the boundaries between paths, beds, and turf. As the grade changes, timbers can be used as steps to make a path more accessible for walking and to control erosion (see the photo below).

A stepped path leads down to a pond. Timber risers control erosion and make the path easier to walk on. (Builder: Kevin Weisgerber.)

BORDER CONSTRUCTION

Borders help a gardener to maintain the landscape by separating diverse elements. For instance, the edge of a lawn can be clearly defined by wood edging (see the photo at right). Without such a barrier, turf must be painstakingly trimmed with a spade. Where slight changes of elevation occur, borders also act as mini-retaining walls, preventing the gradual displacement of soil from, say, a raised flower bed onto a patio.

One of the most important uses of borders is to delineate paths. Although paths can be as informal as a well-worn track through a meadow, hard edging will make a path neater and easier to maintain.

The first step in constructing a border is proper layout. Once location is established, digging a shallow trench will be your next task. In moist, cold climates the trench must then be prepared with filter fabric and gravel to ensure drainage and to prevent frost damage. Then comes the edging itself. And if you want to have a path between the borders, you'll need to surface it.

Laying out the border edge

After you've cleared the area, lay out the edge of your border. For straight lines, stretch strings between stakes. For circular curves, first drive a center stake into the ground and then swing a cord with one end tied to the stake. Tie a rebar pin or a stake to the other end of the cord and scratch a curve in the dirt to define your border. You can lay out irregular curves by flexing a thin wooden batten into position between various points and then marking alongside the batten with spray paint or lime.

A border of landscape timbers separates a bed of tulips from the adjoining lawn.

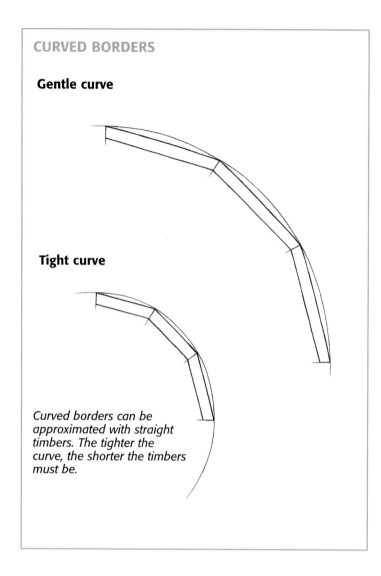

CURVED BORDERS

Gentle curve

Tight curve

Curved borders can be approximated with straight timbers. The tighter the curve, the shorter the timbers must be.

with, and warming it in the sun will increase its flexibility even further. Instead of bending boards into position, you can approximate a curve with straight timbers. The sharper the curve, the shorter the timbers must be (see the drawings at left).

Digging and providing drainage

If you're building a straight border, move the stringline over temporarily by about 2 in. This line will establish where to dig. Leave the original stakes in place. (You will need to restretch the stringline later on as a guide for setting the edging.) Dig a trench along the new stringline location about 4 in. wider than the width of your edging (2 in. on each side).

The depth of the trench depends on your geographical location. In frost-prone regions, edging should be laid on a bed of compacted gravel to promote drainage, so the depth of the trenches should allow for 2 in. to 3 in. of gravel below the edging. When edging is laid directly on dirt, it can be adversely affected by frost heaving (see the sidebar on the facing page). In tropical environments, gravel can be omitted below the edging, but it's still advisable to overdig the trench about 1 in. to allow for a setting bed of compacted sand. The sand makes it easy to level the timbers.

When preparing a path, remove grass and soil from between the border trenches as well so that the surface of the path finishes out at the desired height (a photo essay on building a path with a border begins on p. 81). Stripping topsoil also removes the roots of peren-

If you intend to bend your edging into place, use one of the edging boards to lay out the curve so you can be sure your edging material is flexible enough. If your boards are too stiff to take the bend, switch to a thinner board or lay out a gentler curve. You may want a curved border with more thickness so that you can run a mower wheel on top of it. Consider using a wood/polymer product such as Trex benderboard. Wood/polymer is more flexible than regular lumber to begin

Frost heaving occurs during late fall and early spring when soggy soil freezes and thaws. Freezing causes the soil to expand, thus lifting anything on top of the soil, whether it be a single 4x4 or an entire building. When the ground thaws, the soil settles back down.

If everything were to rise and fall evenly, there would not be a problem. But soil in one spot often lifts more than that in another spot just a few feet away. Expansion may vary from side to side as well, with the soil expanding outward as well as upward. Disparities can be caused by such factors as the angle of the sun throughout the day, the amount of insulating vegetation covering the ground, or differences in soil porosity. As objects on top of the soil get bumped around by this uneven expansion, the wet soil beneath them slumps and shifts. As a result, the wooden border that lined up straight as an arrow last fall may appear lumpy and crooked come spring.

To completely avoid frost heaving, structures must extend below the frost line—the depth at which the ground never freezes. (The frost line varies from a few inches below grade in the deep South to 4 ft. or more in the northern United States and Canada.) Most informal garden structures can tolerate a little unevenness without spoiling their looks, so digging below frost isn't always necessary. Instead, you can place gravel between the structure and the soil to drain water away from the structure. Any water that remains in or around the gravel is free to expand into the spaces between the gravel stones as freezing occurs.

nial weeds. Some landscapers recommend the application of an herbicide at this point as well.

Putting down filter fabric

After digging your trench, lay in strips of synthetic filter fabric. The fabric acts as a root barrier yet allows water to pass through for good drainage. Without filter fabric, topsoil washes into the gravel bed below the edging and prevents the gravel from drawing water away from the edging.

The fabric should extend about 6 in. beyond the outside of the trench (it will be folded tight against the edging later on). After lining the trench, fill it with clean, coarse gravel. Level the gravel with a straightedge and tamp it down with a 4x4 or the end of a sledgehammer.

In the case of a path, fabric should also extend between the two border trenches to discourage the roots of annual weeds from finding moisture in the subsoil below the path. Depending on the width of the path, you may be able to line the path and the trenches with a single wide strip of fabric.

TIMBER EDGING

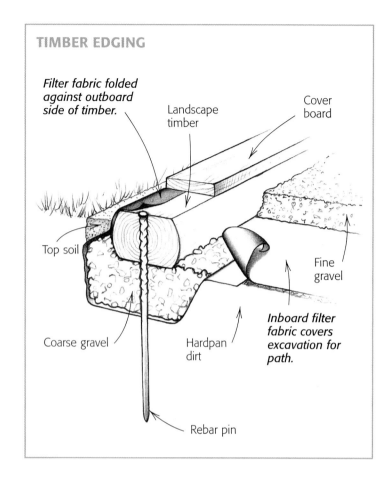

Filter fabric folded against outboard side of timber.

Landscape timber

Cover board

Top soil

Fine gravel

Coarse gravel

Hardpan dirt

Inboard filter fabric covers excavation for path.

Rebar pin

A railroad-tie border keeps soil from drifting onto the adjoining patio.

Installing the edging

Various pressure-treated (PT) products can be used for edging, including square and semisquare timbers. Wide borders such as these are easy to maintain; just run your lawnmower wheel on top of the timber as you mow. For extra-heavy borders, railroad ties work well (see the photo below). You can also use 1x4 boards for thin, almost-invisible borders. An added advantage of these thin boards is their flexibility, allowing them to conform to gentle curves.

Timber edging To install timber edging, reset the stringlines and lay your timbers to the line. Keep the straightest side of each timber on edge for appearance's sake because warped edges are especially noticeable as they're approached along a straight path. Now pin the timbers in place with lengths of rebar or 12-in. spikes (see the drawing at left). Drill clearance holes for the pins a little oversize so that the pins go through easily; otherwise, driving the pins down is liable to push the timber down as well. Drive the pins in place with a sledgehammer, then inspect the border by eyeballing it from one end. If any of the timbers have been knocked sideways, tap them back into position with the sledgehammer.

When installing a border with dirt on both sides, such as between a lawn and a flower bed, hold the fabric in place by adding backfill. After tamping the backfill, trim off the excess fabric with a knife an inch or so above grade level. Now splice the ends of the edging timbers. You can fasten metal truss plates to the sides of adjoining timbers, toenail them together, or use a half-lap splice (for more on joinery options, see p. 42–50).

Another way to splice the edging timbers and hold them in alignment is to use cover boards (which are thin, flat boards placed on top of the edging timbers). If you use cover boards, fold the fabric over the top of the timber before capping to provide an extra measure of protection against weeds. For strength, offset the joints in the cover boards from the joints in the edging timbers by at least 2 ft. Attach the cover boards with galvanized nails or screws.

Board edging Preparation for board edging is essentially the same as for timber edging, except that the trench need not be as wide. Using the same formula for 2 in. of clearance on each side, a 1-in.-thick edging board requires a 5-in.-wide trench. Line the trench with fabric and add gravel (see the drawing at right).

Board edging can be fastened to 1x2 wooden stakes or rebar pins. Keep the stakes or pins on the least-conspicuous side. For instance, when building a typical flower bed/turf border, put your stakes on the flower-bed side, where they can be hidden by mulch. In the case of stakes, drive outdoor screws through the edging into the stake once the stake is in place. Make the stakes from PT yellow pine, even when using cedar or redwood for edging because yellow pine holds screws more tenaciously than cedar or redwood and stands up better under the blows of a sledgehammer.

When using rebar pins, fasten them to edging with galvanized conduit clips (see the photo above and the drawing at right). The clips are sold in different sizes for attaching electrical conduit. The nominal ½-in. size works well with a ⅝-in. rebar pin.

Thin boards create a low-profile edging for this flower bed. The boards are fastened to rebar pins with galvanized conduit clips.

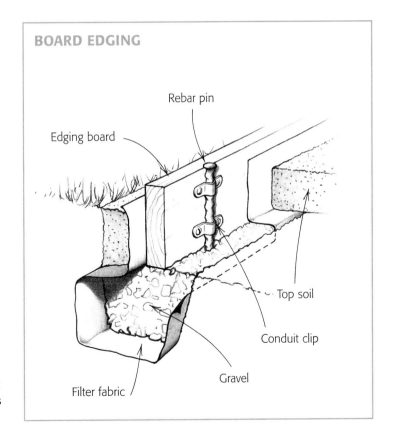

BOARD EDGING

Rebar pin

Edging board

Top soil

Conduit clip

Gravel

Filter fabric

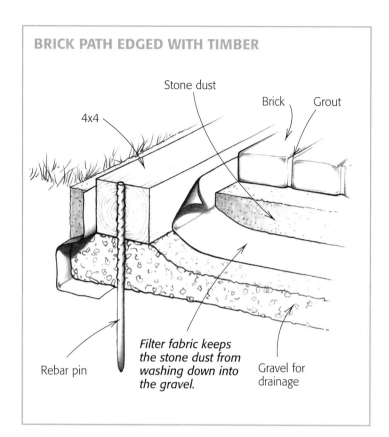

BRICK PATH EDGED WITH TIMBER

Stone dust

Brick   Grout

4x4

Rebar pin

*Filter fabric keeps
the stone dust from
washing down into
the gravel.*

Gravel for
drainage

Surfacing a path

To finish a path, cover the filter fabric with your chosen path material, which could include fine gravel, marble chips, or pine bark. Bark is especially appropriate for woodland settings, while marble chips produce a bright white surface that can really set off adjacent colors. For paths leading directly into the house, use a washed gravel to avoid tracking in dust. In formal settings, a brick path is attractive (see the photo on p. 77). To accommodate bricks, excavate the entire path to the same depth as the border trenches. This will leave room for a bed of stone dust on which to lay the bricks (see the drawing at left).

STEP CONSTRUCTION

Garden steps can be built quickly and relatively cheaply with railroad ties or PT timbers (see the photo at left). The thickness of a railroad tie (7 in.) is very near to the ideal riser height (vertical dimension) used for house steps. So are the dimensions of 8x8 PT timbers, whose actual dimensions run between 7 in. and 8 in. (depending on whether or not they're planed). Surfaced 6x6s, which actually measure 5½ in. square, make for a rather low step, but this may actually suit the pace of a leisurely garden stroll.

With such amenable materials at hand, building landscape steps isn't terribly difficult. But to design steps that are comfortable to ascend and descend, it helps to know some basic theory.

Pitch

The principles governing the design of house stairs also apply to landscape stairs. In either case, the steepness of a

Pressure-treated 8x8s have been stacked to make a set of steps. The low-voltage light fastened to the lowermost riser illuminates the path in the foreground. (Builder: Kevin Weisgerber.)

staircase is expressed as pitch, which is the ratio of the stair's overall height to its overall width (see the drawing at right). For instance, a staircase might rise 7 ft. vertically between the bottom step and the top step while traversing a horizontal distance of 10 ft. Each individual step would be a sort of microcosm of the entire staircase, having a riser height of 7 in. and a tread width (horizontal dimension) of 10 in. In both cases, the pitch is expressed as the ratio 7:10.

Stairs that are too steep are exhausting to climb and dangerous to descend. On the other hand, stairs that rise too slowly can be tedious, requiring an awkward shuffle. The optimum pitch for stairs is about 7:10. Accordingly, a straight set of landscape steps imposed on a hillside with a 7:10 pitch would be comfortable to climb. In the natural world, of course, hillsides with 7:10 pitch are the exceptions rather than the rule, so you may have to build your stairs on a difficult slope. Let's look at the simple case first, then tackle the harder one.

Steps that follow the slope

To build a straight stepped path, say across a lawn and down to a pond, begin by laying out the path with stakes and stringlines. Starting at the bottom of the path, set the first riser (cross timber) in a shallow bed of compacted gravel. Cut half-lap joints on the ends of this first riser to accept mating half laps on the first pair of stringers (side timbers). Succeeding steps won't require half laps because both riser and stringer have a step below to which they can be spiked (see the top drawing on p. 76).

Butt one end of each stringer into a riser in front, with the other end buried into the slope. The stringer must extend back far enough to provide a solid foun-

dation for the next riser. To determine this, set one end of a level on the first riser and move the other end of the level up or down the slope until the

(see the top drawing on p. 76).

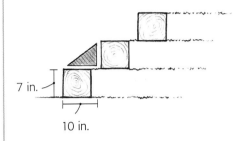

DEFINING PITCH

Pitch is a way of measuring slope, expressed as the ratio of vertical rise to horizontal travel. All three of the conditions below have a 7:10 pitch.

The ratio of a 7-in. stair riser to a 10-in. stair tread

7 in.

10 in.

The ratio of a staircase's 7-ft. height to its 10-ft. breadth

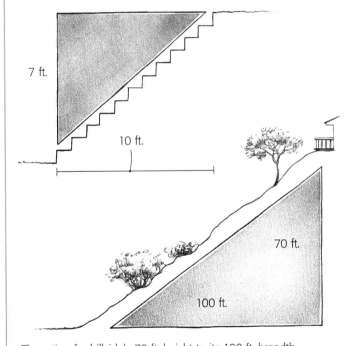

7 ft.

10 ft.

70 ft.

100 ft.

The ratio of a hillside's 70-ft. height to its 100-ft. breadth

LANDSCAPE STEPS

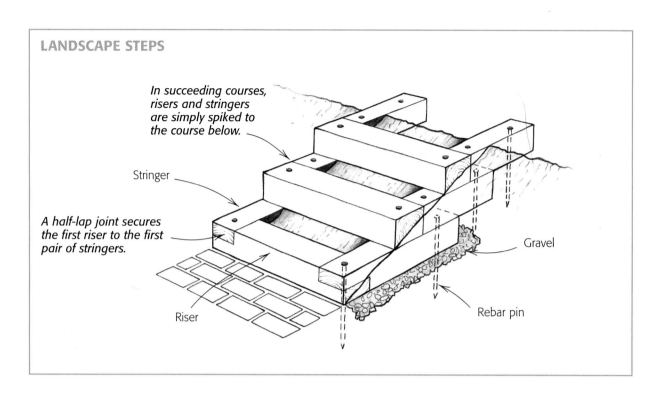

In succeeding courses, risers and stringers are simply spiked to the course below.

Stringer

A half-lap joint secures the first riser to the first pair of stringers.

Riser

Gravel

Rebar pin

LEVELING STRINGERS

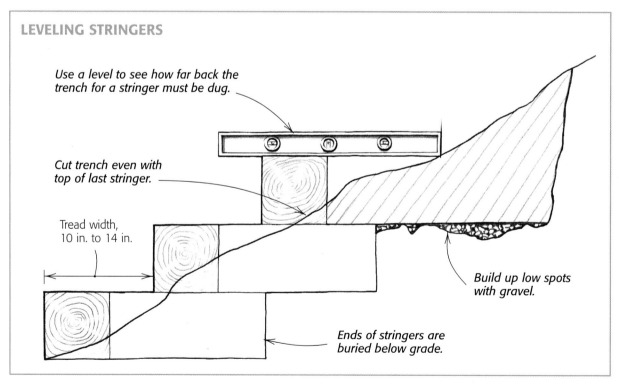

Use a level to see how far back the trench for a stringer must be dug.

Cut trench even with top of last stringer.

Tread width, 10 in. to 14 in.

Build up low spots with gravel.

Ends of stringers are buried below grade.

bubble reads true (centered in the vial). This is about where the front of the next riser will be located. Dig past this point at least another foot and lay a few inches of gravel in the trench.

The rough tolerances found in landscape steps mean that a little frost action under the stringers won't be a problem. The exceptions are the top and bottom steps, where alignment with other surfaces may be important. If you live in a frost-prone region and you want to prevent all threats of frost heaving, overdig all of the trenches, add gravel, and lay all the stringers on top of the gravel.

Set the first stringers in place and drill through the half-lap joints at each end. Drive 2-ft. lengths of rebar through the joints and down into the ground. Pin the opposite (soon to be buried) ends to the earth also. Then lay the second riser across the stringers and spike it in position. Use the level to determine how deep the next pair of side trenches should extend (see the bottom drawing on the facing page). Scrape these trenches level with the top surfaces of the preceding stringers before you install the stringers. This will keep the stringers level with the previous steps. If you overdig, build the bottom of the trench back up with gravel or compacted earth.

After spiking the second pair of stringers to the first pair (and to the slope), set the third riser. Continue in this fashion until you reach the top of the path. The treads should all be the same width so that people won't trip. (More on determining tread width in the next section.) Backfill the completed stairs with earth or a hard-packing aggregate such as crusher run. The surface of the steps can also be paved with cobbles or cordwood pavers (2-in.-thick wooden disks crosscut from the end of a

These steps are paved with brick and edged with 6x6s. The tread surfaces are pitched downhill for good drainage. The brick pattern is called basket weave.

log). A formal effect is achieved by using brick infill (see the photo above).

Steps for difficult slopes

The slope of most garden landscapes is lower than the ideal stair pitch of 7:10. Although the rules for indoor stairs are quite strict, the rules for outdoor stairs are more flexible because people are more careful when stepping outside. That means you can deviate from the 7:10 standard to accommodate a gently rising slope. A riser/tread ratio as low as 7:14 would be acceptable in the garden. Don't make the tread less than 10 in. wide, or people will be likely to trip.

As the width of the tread increases, the stride of the person using the stairs gets stretched as well. For slopes lower than 7:14, it's better to build up the stairway into level terraces connected by two or three standard 7:10 steps (see the drawing on p. 80). The length of each terrace should be close to a multiple of 20 in. (i.e., 20 in., 40 in., 60 in.), which will locate the next riser in a convenient location for the average person. It's

A portable circular saw takes much of the exertion out of carpentry—it can cut through a 2x4 in about two seconds. But this tool is also dangerous because it can cut through a hand or finger just as easily. Because there's no way to react quickly enough to avert an accident, it's essential that the tool be used safely at all times.

A circular saw is among the noisiest and dustiest of all power tools, so wear ear and eye protection when using one. You'll also need to protect against kickback—one of the primary hazards of using a circular saw. Kickback usually occurs when a board isn't set up properly for cutting. As you make the cut, the two parts of the board sag toward each other, pinching the sawblade, which causes the blade to come to a sudden halt and kick back.

To prevent kickback, make sure that the part of the board being cut off is free to fall away. When trimming off a small amount, just let the end stick out over your sawhorse. When you're cutting through the middle of a board, however, stabilize this setup by placing a weight (such as a concrete block) on the fixed end. As you approach the end of the cut, follow through with a swift, steady push. Otherwise, the weight of the falling piece is liable to split off a part of the remaining board. To guard against surprises, always stand slightly to one side of the cutline. If the saw kicks back, it will go into midair rather than into your groin. Also, be sure that the spring-loaded blade guard is functioning properly. If it sticks, try spraying it with a penetrating lubricant such as WD-40.

The depth of cut of the saw should be set so that the blade sticks out below the bottom of a board by about the length of one tooth. Putting more blade in the cut just increases friction. Most jobs require an angle adjustment of 90°. Check this occasionally with a square, especially if your

SUPPORTING STOCK

Cutting between supports is wrong. The board pinches the blade—pow!

butt joints don't seem to be fitting tightly. Angle cuts (bevels) are also possible by tilting the saw's shoe.

Cutting operations can be divided into crosscutting (across the grain), ripping (with the grain), and plywood cutting. To start a freehand cut, align both the sawblade and the guide notch on the saw's shoe with your cutline. (Some saws have two guide notches—one for 90° cuts and one for 45° bevel cuts.) Back the saw away from the board a little before hitting the trigger. Once you start cutting, it will be hard to watch the blade because so much sawdust will be flying, so steer the saw by the guide notch instead.

You can obtain more accuracy by using cutting guides. For crosscutting, you can hold a Speed Square against the work to guide the saw. To rip multiple pieces of the same width, use a rip guide. To adjust the rip guide, flip the saw on its back and set the correct distance between the

guide's fence and the sawblade. (Make sure the saw is unplugged.)

Circular sawblades come in many patterns, but for landscape carpentry all you really need is a good 24-tooth combination blade. (The word "combination" means that it will work equally well for rips, crosscuts, and miters.) Carbide-tipped blades are worth the extra money because of their durability, although a sharp steel-tipped blade cuts just as well, if not better. Special blades for cutting treated wood are available with a nonstick coating, which fights the extra friction caused by wet PT lumber.

As a sawblade becomes dull, it will cut slower, make more noise, and produce a burning smell. Eventually the heat generated by dull teeth will cause the blade to warp, causing even more friction, and finally making the blade unusable. Don't let the situation go this far—it increases the risk of kickback and causes premature wear and tear on the tool.

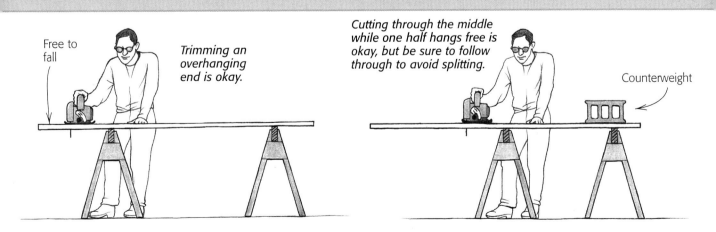

Free to fall

Trimming an overhanging end is okay.

Cutting through the middle while one half hangs free is okay, but be sure to follow through to avoid splitting.

Counterweight

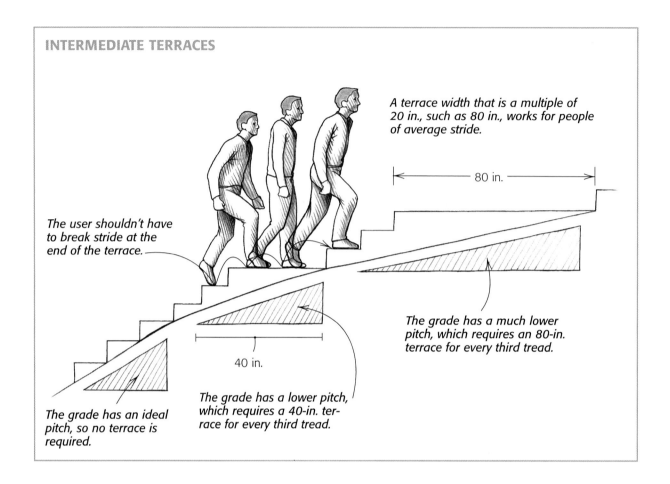

A terrace width that is a multiple of 20 in., such as 80 in., works for people of average stride.

80 in.

The user shouldn't have to break stride at the end of the terrace.

The grade has a much lower pitch, which requires an 80-in. terrace for every third tread.

40 in.

The grade has a lower pitch, which requires a 40-in. terrace for every third tread.

The grade has an ideal pitch, so no terrace is required.

annoying and dangerous to have to shorten or lengthen one's stride as a riser approaches, especially with a bag of groceries under each arm. If you're exceptionally short or tall, you may want to mock up the length of a proposed terrace to see how it works with your stride. If the slope of the hillside changes over the course of the stairs, add or subtract risers as needed to lengthen or shorten the next terrace.

Intermittent terraces in a set of steps do more than just create an acceptable stair pitch. They also give the user a breather between flights of steps, in the same way that an intermediate landing does with an interior staircase.

While slopes that are too gentle can be terraced upward without too much difficulty, hillsides that are too steep present a tougher problem. One way to build a comfortable stair here is to cut into the hillside. At that point, something must be done to keep the sides of the cut from collapsing. If heavy equipment is available, the easiest solution may be to slope back the sides of the cut to the point where plantings will hold the soil in place. Another option would be to build a pair of timber flank walls alongside the staircase (see pp. 93–96). Timber risers can be easily woven into these flank walls to produce a staircase.

BUILDING A PATH WITH BORDER

Borders separate two materials. Sometimes that means separating a garden from the grass beyond. In other cases it means outlining a path so that the path material stays separate from the adjoining lawn or planting bed. The path in the pages to follow is easy to build because it's filled with gravel. If you want a more formal look, though, you can build the same borders and change your infill material to brick. The same approach shown here for double borders along a path applies to a single border used to define a garden.

Careful preparation is the key to success for borders and paths. A gravel subbase helps drain water away after a rain and prevents the frost heaving that can dislodge your border timbers. Filter fabric keeps fine soil particles from infiltrating into the gravel bed, thereby preserving the gravel's draining effect. Fabric also acts as a weed barrier.

These 4x4 border timbers are capped with cover boards, which help tie the 4x4s together and hold them in alignment. The high-grade material used for the cover boards hides defects in the rougher-grade timbers below. A wide border such as this affords easy tracking for a lawnmower, but if you want a low-profile look you can switch to thin boards set on edge.

(continued on page 82)

1 Set up stringlines 2 in. outside of the intended location of the border timbers. Dig the path to a depth about equal to the thickness of the border timber. Then carefully trim back the turf to the line.

2 Dig side trenches for the border timbers an extra 2 in. to 3 in. deep to make room for gravel.

3 Line the excavation with filter fabric and fill the side trenches with coarse gravel. Level the gravel bed using a long, straight 2x4.

4 Reset the guide stringlines and pin the timbers in position with lengths of rebar. Drill clearance holes in the timbers so that the rebar penetrates easily.

5 Fill the path with pea gravel, then wrap filter fabric over the top of the timber and staple it in place.

6 Trim any excess filter fabric away with a utility knife, then nail the cover board on top of border timber.

7 Spread and level the pea gravel with an iron rake, then compact it with a tamper. Finally, backfill against the outsides of the timbers with topsoil.

6 Retaining Walls

Hillsides present the gardener with a mixed blessing. Aesthetically, steep slopes can add movement and drama to a landscape. In practical terms, however, they are a challenge—difficult to stand on, difficult to walk on, and difficult to cultivate. And when a hillside's ground cover is disturbed by cultivation, the exposed topsoil is liable to wash away, leaving an ugly outcropping of stones and roots.

To make a hillside stable and accessible, it can be terraced with a series of wood retaining walls. (A photo essay on building a retaining wall begins on p. 93.) To design a terraced landscape, you'll need to determine the number, height, and configuration of the terrace(s). Environmental factors must be taken into account, such as exposure to wind and sun, as well as practical requirements, such as the need for building space. The job's level of difficulty will also be affected by your decisions. A retaining wall of any kind involves the moving of a lot of heavy stuff, so it pays to consider all the design options up front.

As far as the actual building of wood retaining walls is concerned, there's literally more to it than meets the eye. That's because buried timbers are used to anchor retaining walls to the earth behind them. This anchoring enables a wall to withstand the tremendous pressure generated by wet or frozen earth. To keep this pressure to a minimum, drainage must be assured through careful preparation and proper backfilling.

RETAINING-WALL DESIGN

You'll have to address two major issues when you design a retaining wall. One is the size of the terrace created above the wall. The second is the wall's relationship to the hillside on which it stands. A wall can be fully recessed into a hill, built entirely on top of it, or a combination of both.

This tall retaining wall has been backfilled to create a broad terrace. Notice the tubing installed at the base of the wall to provide drainage. (Builder: Peter Kreyling; photo by Peter Kreyling.)

Terrace size

The size and number of terraces is the designer's first decision (see the drawing at right). At one extreme, you can wall off an entire slope, creating a single large terrace. A large terrace may be more useful than several smaller ones, especially when a major feature such as a patio or an outbuilding must be accommodated. On lots that are steeply sloped, tall retaining walls may be the only way to create necessary space.

The problem with creating one large terrace is that it maximizes the building effort involved. As the height of a wall increases, the loads it must withstand also increase (see sidebar on p. 86). Consequently, the wall must be not only bigger but also stronger, which means

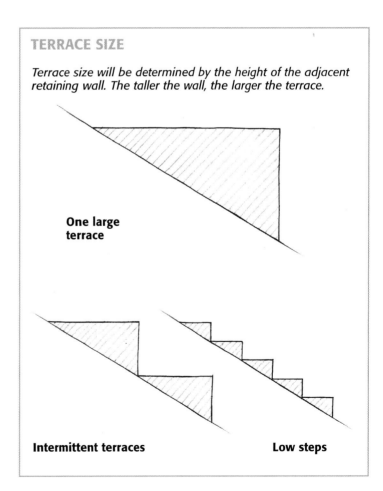

TERRACE SIZE

Terrace size will be determined by the height of the adjacent retaining wall. The taller the wall, the larger the terrace.

One large terrace

Intermittent terraces

Low steps

Retaining walls must withstand terrific pressure from the earth they hold back. While dry soil exerts a lot of weight, to some extent a pile of dry earth is self supporting. On the other hand, when soil is saturated with water, it becomes semi-liquid. That's when the real test begins.

To grasp the problem, think of a bag of rice. In its dry state, the rice can easily be contained in a thin plastic bag. But if you soak that rice in water, it becomes heavier, and the water acts as a lubricant so that the grains of rice slide more easily against each other. After a while, the rice starts to swell and the bag finally bursts. Multiply this scenario a few thousand times, and you get some idea of the pressure acting on a retaining wall after a rainstorm.

In the winter, the problem worsens. As wet ground freezes, ice causes the soil to expand even more. Once a retaining wall is kicked outward by frozen ground, it

stays that way; as temperatures rise, thawed-out soil settles into the wedge-shaped void left between the earth and the back of the wall. There's only one way to repair this: reconstruct the wall.

Since groundwater is the nemesis of every retaining wall, the most important consideration in retaining-wall design is drainage. Good drainage begins with a gravel-filled trench at the base of the wall (see the drawing on the facing page). For gravel, use a clean, coarse crushed stone such as a #57 (#57 is stone-yard terminology for gravel stones about 1 in. long).

On the bottom of the trench place a perforated plastic drainage tube and surround it with gravel. Be sure to specify perforated tubing because a solid-wall variety is also available. The drainage tube must extend to some convenient drop-off point, such as a dry well, an underground storm drain, or daylight (any point at grade level down-

using heavier timbers, larger fasteners, and more tiebacks (anchoring timbers).

A single large terrace also requires a lot more digging or filling than a succession of smaller ones, so heavy equipment is almost certainly necessary. Because of these construction challenges, retaining walls over 5 ft. tall are best left to licensed, insured contractors and should never be attempted without first consulting a structural engineer.

But instead of one big terrace, you can sculpt a slope into a series of smaller terraces (see the photo on p. 88). The width of each terrace should provide for a comfortable path, as well as for any planting beds that are desired. This scheme looks more natural than one large, overbearing grade change and requires less work. If the grade isn't too steep and you don't need too wide an area, a series of low walls is your best bet.

hill from the wall). Local building codes prohibit the emptying of groundwater into sanitary sewers. When laying the drain, be sure that its holes face down; otherwise, large dirt particles and other trash could enter the drain, causing it to clog.

A buffer of filter fabric and a 1-ft. wall of gravel should come between the back of the wall and any soil. As water seeps out of the soil into the gravel buffer, it runs down between the stones, finding its way to the perforated drain. With this drainage, the hydrostatic pressure behind the wall never builds up to the danger level.

In addition to reducing pressure on your wall, rapid drainage benefits plantings. In turn, the roots of shrubs and ground covers help bind the soil and further alleviate pressure. Don't place trees too close to a retaining wall, however, since large roots can exert destructive pressures of their own.

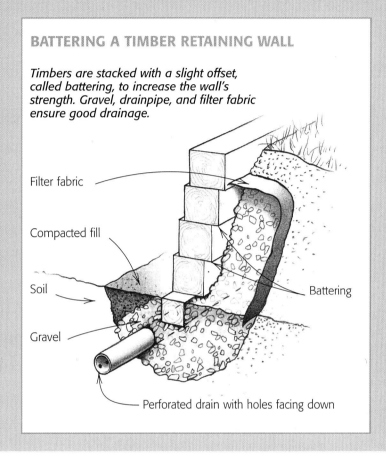

BATTERING A TIMBER RETAINING WALL

Timbers are stacked with a slight offset, called battering, to increase the wall's strength. Gravel, drainpipe, and filter fabric ensure good drainage.

Filter fabric

Compacted fill

Soil

Gravel

Battering

Perforated drain with holes facing down

To keep the look even more natural, you can terrace a gentle slope to create actual steps, with each "retaining wall" consisting of a single timber. This technique stabilizes a slope with a minimum of effort. However, the width of the resulting terraces may be too narrow for practical purposes, especially on a steep grade.

Digging options

The second decision in retaining-wall design is whether to cut into a bank, add fill on top of it, or do a combination of both (see the drawing on p. 88). Cutting into a bank completely means that the resulting terrace is fully recessed below the surface of the hillside. Retaining walls will be required to hold back the remaining earth at the back and sides of the terrace. The opposite

Terraces can be built on top of grade, below grade, or by a combination of both.

Terrace recessed below grade

Terrace built on top of grade with fill dirt

Terrace partially recessed below grade using removed dirt as fill

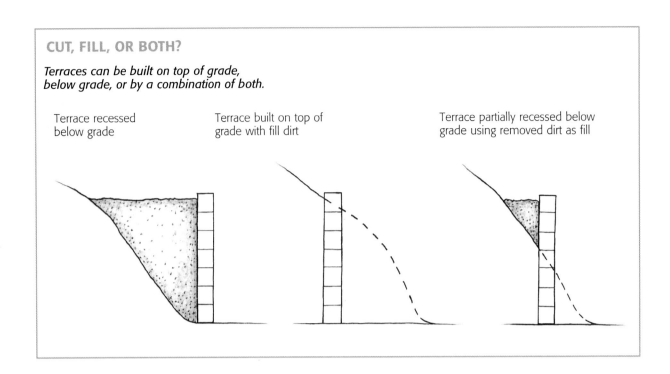

A series of low retaining walls has been used to terrace this steep site. Boulders have been incorporated into the lowermost course to achieve a natural look. (Builder: Kevin Weisgerber.)

approach is to build a retaining wall above grade and then fill in behind it. A middle course is to cut away part of the bank, build a wall at the back of the cut, and then use the removed dirt to fill in behind the wall.

Recessed terrace A fully recessed terrace has an enclosed, intimate feeling similar to a courtyard garden in town. A wind-sheltered space such as this can extend summer's warmth by a few weeks on both ends. Because the terrace consists of recessed wing walls flanking a main wall in back, the view from the terrace is directed to the front, which could be an advantage or disadvantage depending on local scenery. As with city gardens, the choice of plants here may be affect-ed by a limited exposure to sunlight, and of course you must consider what to do with all the fill dirt generated by digging this type of terrace.

Fastening Wood with Rebar

Lengths of concrete reinforcing bar (rebar) are useful for spiking heavy timbers and logs together. They're also used to pin timbers to the earth, such as for borders and retaining walls. Rebar is typically sold in 20-ft. lengths, but precut lengths of 12 in., 18 in., and 24 in. may be available. For corrosion resistance, try to find galvanized rebar or galvanized spikes instead of ordinary rebar. Some suppliers will custom-cut rebar for you on a special shear, or with an oxy-acetylene torch.

If you need to cut rebar on the job site, use a hacksaw or an abrasive metal-cutting blade mounted in a circular saw. After cutting about three quarters of the way through, bend the bar back and forth to snap the piece in two.

You don't need to form a point on the end of a rebar "pin," as long as you drill a clearance hole through both timbers. A head on one end is also unnecessary because the rough surface of rebar pins causes them to hold well.

Use a circular saw equipped with an abrasive wheel to cut rebar.

Built-up terrace To create a built-up terrace, you can build your retaining wall entirely on top of the existing grade and fill in behind it, provided that you heave enough fill dirt and an access road to get it to your wall location. A built-up terrace has a raised, airy feeling. The view is extended on all sides, and the area receives lots of sunlight. Welcome breezes are found here in summer, but so are chill winds in autumn and spring.

Cut and filled terrace To avoid importing or exporting fill dirt, you can recess your retaining wall halfway into a bank and use the excavated dirt and rock to fill in behind the wall. If you have no way to bring in trucks or digging equipment to the site, this is the most practical option.

RETAINING-WALL CONSTRUCTION

Pressure–treated (PT) timbers (6x6 or 8x8), railroad ties, and semisquare landscape timbers are commonly used for retaining walls. Square PT timbers create the cleanest, most geometric look. Railroad ties have a rougher appearance, and their dark color helps them recede into the background. Semisquare land-scape timbers have the most texture of the three, as well as a rustic, backwoods connotation.

Masonry walls rely largely on their own weight to resist the pressure of the soil behind them, but wood retaining walls are lighter, so they must be anchored to the adjoining earth. When anchoring is ignored, you end up with a leaning, bulging wall.

Installing tiebacks

To anchor wood retaining walls effec-tively, use buried timbers, called tiebacks. Tiebacks run roughly perpen-dicular to the face of the wall and are placed every 8 ft. or so. Tiebacks should reach back far enough to provide plenty of soil weight on top of them and should be positioned deep in the lower courses, rather than just below the sur-face, for the same reason. There are sev-eral ways to secure tiebacks into a slope, and the methods can be used separately or in combination with each other (see the drawings at left).

The first method is to pin tiebacks into undisturbed soil using 2–ft. lengths of reinforcing bar (called rebar). This method is effective as long as the soil is hard enough and the tiebacks reach back far enough. For a more secure way to anchor a wood retaining wall, create a strong framework, called a crib, behind the exposed wall. At the back of the crib, stack cross ties between the tiebacks in log–cabin fashion. When the crib is buried with gravel and dirt, the weight of the backfill supports the wall.

For a more economical alternative to the full–crib design, spike short blocks to the ends of individual tiebacks. The resulting "T" configuration works like a ship's anchor to hook each tieback into the embankment.

Battering

To alleviate pressure at the top of the wall, it helps to "batter" the wall's face by offsetting each course of timbers by ¾ in. to produce a backward tilt (see the photo at right). The resulting flare at the bottom of the wall has a buttressing effect, helping to support the earth behind the wall. Besides being stronger, a battered wall has a more solid look than a wall with a truly vertical face. Also, offsetting the timbers lends a tex–ture to the wall's finished surface.

Building the wall

The first step is to dig a trench and install the gravel bed (for more on this, see the sidebar on pp. 86–87). Lay the first course (or layer) of timber in the gravel bed below grade to help keep the wall in place. To keep the first course from sliding forward, place well–compacted backfill against it on the out–side of the wall.

The first two to three courses of tim–ber can be laid without any tiebacks. Be sure to stagger end joints by at least 4 ft. to avoid weak spots in the wall. To fas–ten timbers together, drive galvanized spikes or rebar pins (for more on work–ing with rebar, see the sidebar on p. 89)

Battering gives this timber retaining wall tex-ture and a solid look. A blue-gray stain helps the wall blend into its surroundings.

into predrilled holes in the timbers. Locate the spikes 6 in. from each end and every 3 ft. or so in between.

As the third course is being laid, install the first tiebacks. Cut pockets into the slope to receive the buried end of each tieback and spike the tiebacks to the wall in front and to the earth in back. The next course consists of more wall timbers in front and cross ties or T-blocks in back. Instead of splicing cross ties end to end on the tieback, stagger them so that both timbers get a good purchase on the tieback.

Use the same alternating pattern until you reach the second–to–last course, when you no longer need to use tiebacks. Once the timber work is com-plete, pour in the gravel backfill.

How a retaining wall terminates depends on its relationship to the adjoining hillside (see the drawings on p. 92). If the wall cuts all the way across

*Retaining walls can be terminated in different ways,
depending on the surrounding topography.*

Tapered end wall

Recessed wall

Built-up wall

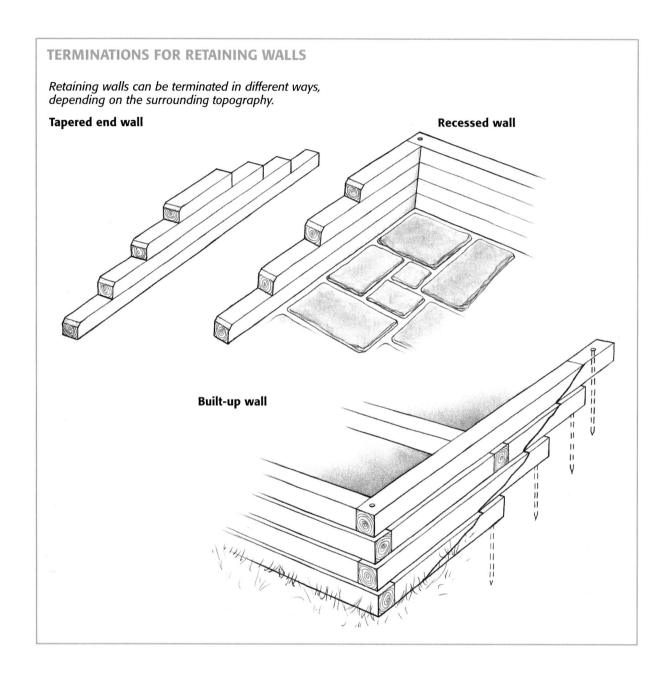

a hill, its ends will simply taper down to grade in succeeding courses. With a terrace recessed into a hillside, the wing walls step down to grade in similar fashion, while the main wall is interlocked with the wing walls in log-cabin fashion. When a terrace is built out from a hillside, the wing-wall timbers step up rather than down, with their ends buried into the slope. The installation in this last case is similar to burying stair stringers (see p. 75). Pin each course in the wing wall to the slope with rebar, and tie any buried cribbing into the wing walls as well for strength.

Compared to masonry walls, timber walls such as this one are quick and inexpensive. Wood retaining walls are not complicated to build, but they do require lots of digging and lifting. This wall incorporates stairs to provide access to the level above the wall. You can use railroad ties or PT timbers for this project, but be sure that the timbers are rated for ground contact because they will be partially buried. You can fill the steps in with the same materials you would use for paths.

Your biggest concern for this project will be drainage, which means laying drainage tubing and backfilling with gravel (see the sidebar on pp. 86-87). The best way to strengthen a timber retaining wall is with tiebacks (see p. 90). This six-course wall is about as high as you would typically build on your own. Higher walls encounter greater soil pressures and require lots of heavy earth moving, so you'd probably need to hire a professional for the job.

(continued on page 94)

1 Dig trenches for main wall (foreground) and wing wall (left).

2 Line the trench with filter fabric and spread a thin layer of gravel on top. Then lay perforated drainage tubing in the trench with the holes facing down.

3 Cover the tubing with gravel and lay a base course of timber in position. Use a 4-ft. spirit level to set the timber level.

4 Shovel in compacted top soil to fill the front of the trench. It should finish flush with the top of the base course of timber.

5 To determine the extent of the cut for the first stair stringer, place a scrap of timber on the base course. With the scrap to simulate the stringer, use a level to carry the height of the stringer over to the hillside. Mark the far end of the cut with spray paint.

6 Dig a trench for the stringer and place gravel in the bottom so the top of the gravel bed is flush with the top of the base course of timbers. Then mark the length of the stringer in place, as shown here, or take a measurement to cut the stringer. This is the same process to follow for all succeeding stringers.

7 Drill the first stair stringer in preparation for spiking it to the base course.

8 Spike the second riser to a stringer. This stringer will become a part of the flank wall, which terminates the retaining wall. Continue on with the rest of the courses in the same way.

9 Use a framing square in conjunction with a level to lay out the digging for the first tieback.

10 Pin the first tieback to the hillside with rebar.

11 Fasten cross ties to the buried ends of the tiebacks in the preceding course. Here, a single cross tie spans the entire width of the wall, with its ends tied into the flank walls.

12 Continue building the wall until you reach the sixth course, which completes the wall.

Raised Beds

Properly cultivated raised beds can produce a maximum harvest in a minimum amount of growing space. In Europe, where land has been a scarce commodity for centuries, raised beds have long been popular. In the post–World War II years, as Americans moved to the suburbs, the raised–bed concept spoke to the need for a compact, pro-ductive garden in a neat package. About the same time, interest in gourmet cooking acquainted gardeners with the French Intensive method of gardening, in which raised beds play an important role. Today, raised beds have sprung up in backyards across America. Urban gardeners, as well, have claimed raised beds, using them to transform terraces and rooftops into miniature Edens.

Raised beds can be built from many different types of lumber. They also employ different methods for countering the pressure generated by contained soil. Soil pressure can cause a raised bed to bulge in the middle, or, worse yet, to split apart at the corners. One type of raised bed uses stakes to resist soil pressure. Other types depend on wood or metal cross ties to hold them together in the middle.

A raised bed of landscape timbers tumbles gaily down a slope.

SPACING OF STAKES OR CROSS TIES FOR RAISED BED

Nominal thickness of side boards	Actual thickness of sideboards	Spacing of intermediate stakes or cross ties*	
		PT yellow pine or PT Douglas fir	Redwood, cedar, or cypress
5/4x	1 in.	3 ft.	2 ft.
2x	1½ in.	4 ft.	3 ft.
4x	3½ in.	8 ft.	6 ft.
6x	5½ in.	12 ft.	10 ft.

*This is also the maximum length of the raised bed if no intermediate supports are used.

This vertical timber bed provides an oasis in the middle of a paved courtyard.

DESIGNING A RAISED BED

The gardener's reach should determine the width of a raised bed. The standard width is 4 ft. to 5 ft., which requires a 2-ft. to 2½-ft. reach from both sides. A bed narrower than this won't provide much tillable area after deducting the thickness of the bed's sides. The bed can be as long as you like, provided you use enough stakes or cross ties to keep the sides from spreading (see the chart above). If you don't want any stakes or cross ties, the length of the bed will be limited by the strength of the sides.

The height of the bed will be a compromise between the gardener's back muscles, calling for a higher bed, and outward-thrusting soil pressure, which increases exponentially as the height of a bed rises. Also, filling even a small bed with dirt is a big job, especially if you have to dig it up from somewhere else. An ample raised-bed height would be 15 in. to 19 in., requiring a pair of 2x8s or a pair of 2x10s, respectively, as side boards. Lower beds made from a single 2x12 also work well, as long as the soil placed in the bed is complemented by friable native soil below.

Wood choices

Although nominal 2-in.-thick pressure-treated (PT) lumber is the most common material for a raised bed, you can use other thicknesses as well. Thinner materials such as 5/4x6 (pronounced five-

Is Pressure-Treated Lumber Safe for Raised Beds?

Ideally, a raised bed should be filled with a soil mix rich in organic matter and teeming with worms and microbial activity. Needless to say, this is no place for wood that's prone to decay. Pressure-treated (PT) lumber seems like the ideal material for a raised bed. Not only is it guaranteed against rot, but the species most widely treated, southern yellow pine, has the strength needed to withstand soil pressures. For vegetable gardeners, however, the troublesome caveat associated with PT lumber is the specter of soil contamination.

PT lumber contains copper, chromium, and arsenic (CCA), all of which are poisonous to some degree (see pp. 27-29). In theory, leaching of these elements should not occur, because CCA is bound to the wood's cell structure as an "insoluble metal complex." On the other hand, nobody claims that PT lumber will last forever, so what happens in 20, 30, or 40 years, when the stuff finally starts to rot?

In all probability, the constant watering of a raised bed, combined with the friable soil structure of its contents, would wash away trace amounts of CCA long before they reached toxic levels. For peace of mind, however, you might want to opt for a naturally decay-resistant wood, such as construction-grade redwood, when building a raised vegetable bed, even if its life span is limited to 10 or 15 years.

---

quarter by six) will require more stakes or cross ties to compensate for the reduction in strength compared to 2x. Nominal 1–in. lumber, which actually measures only ¾ in. in thickness, isn't really strong enough for a raised bed.

If you're planting edibles, you may want to avoid PT lumber and build your raised bed from a naturally decay–resistant species, such as redwood, cedar, or cypress (for more on the safety of PT lumber, see the sidebar above). These woods aren't as strong as yellow pine or Douglas fir, the two most commonly treated species, so you'll need to place stakes or cross ties closer together.

If there's a sawmill nearby, look into the possibility of using green lumber.

These raised beds of pressure-treated lumber have hoops for removable cloches.

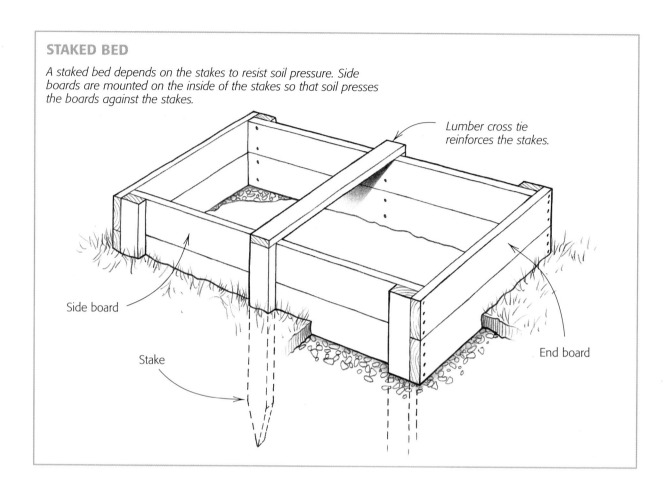

A staked bed depends on the stakes to resist soil pressure. Side boards are mounted on the inside of the stakes so that soil presses the boards against the stakes.

Lumber cross tie reinforces the stakes.

Side board

Stake

End board

There's no point in buying seasoned lumber for a raised bed, where ground moisture will always be present.

Staked beds

Staking the sides of a raised bed transfers outward-thrusting forces to the subsoil below (see the drawing on the facing page). This is a simple and inexpensive way to reinforce a raised bed, but a lot depends on the soil in your area. Marshy soil is too soft to hold stakes securely. At the other extreme, some soil is so rocky that it's practically impossible to drive a stake into it. Stakes work best in firm, homogenous clay, so if you're building over this type of sub-

soil, a staked bed is a good choice (for more on building a staked bed, see the photo essay on p. 106).

Stakes need to be driven well below grade for strength. They should penetrate 1½ ft. to 2½ ft. into hard, undisturbed subsoil. If you plan to cultivate the soil below the bed, leave a 6-in.-wide strip of undisturbed soil around the edges to avoid weakening your stakes.

PT 2x4 stakes work well in soil that's not too rocky. Cut a long tapering angle on the ends of the stakes for easy penetration. Point the stakes with a circular saw, being sure to clamp them securely to a pair of sawhorses before cutting. It's easier to point both ends of a long piece and then cut it in half, producing two stakes.

You don't need to dig holes before driving stakes, but if the soil is very hard, stab the ground a few times with a digging bar to give the stake a head start in the right direction.

In rocky soils, it's difficult to drive a stake with any kind of accuracy. When the stake hits a rock, it veers off and tilts out of plumb. To some extent, it's possible to pound the stake back on course and continue, but if you're among boulders, a wooden stake will shatter before you reach the necessary depth. For rocky situations, you may be able to use galvanized steel pipe, which can take more of a beating than wooden stakes. Use at least 1-in.-diameter pipes for strength and to provide a significant bearing surface against the soil. Slender lengths of rebar can be driven easily enough, but they are too flexible to perform well as stakes, and their narrow profile is apt to cut through the subsoil rather than bear against it.

Side boards should be placed on the soil side of the stakes rather than on the outside so the weight of the soil holds the boards against the stakes. Wooden stakes should be attached to side boards with galvanized screws or nails, while pipe stakes should be attached with galvanized conduit clips. The nails, screws, or conduit clips used to fasten side boards to the stakes actually become superfluous once the bed is filled and soil pressure takes over. If side boards are placed on the outside of the stakes, soil pressure will be constantly working to push them away from the stakes. Because this arrangement conceals the stakes, however, it may be preferable for aesthetic reasons. In that case, fasten the

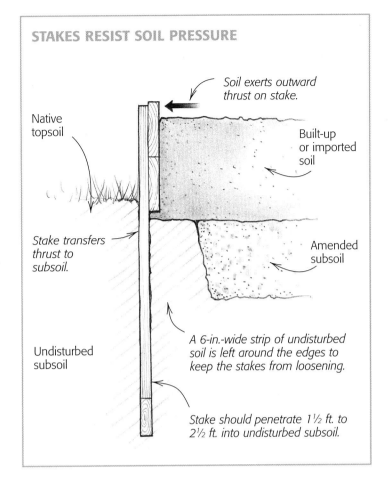

STAKES RESIST SOIL PRESSURE

Soil exerts outward thrust on stake.

Native topsoil

Built-up or imported soil

Stake transfers thrust to subsoil.

Amended subsoil

Undisturbed subsoil

A 6-in.-wide strip of undisturbed soil is left around the edges to keep the stakes from loosening.

Stake should penetrate 1½ ft. to 2½ ft. into undisturbed subsoil.

side boards to the stakes with through-bolts instead of with nails or screws.

Although stakes keep the sides of a raised bed from bowing out, for additional insurance, you can tie the tops of opposing stakes together with a 2x4 cross tie. By attaching the cross tie to the stakes with screws rather than nails, it can be removed temporarily when it's time to turn the garden over in spring or fall. The rest of the time, you can save your back by leaning an elbow on the nearest cross tie while thinning or weeding.

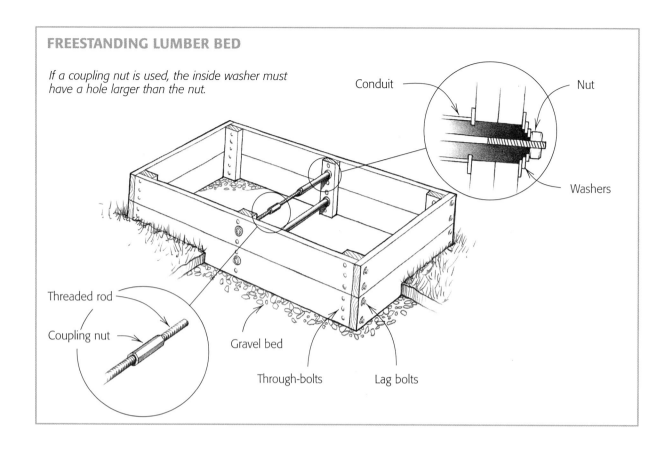

FREESTANDING LUMBER BED

If a coupling nut is used, the inside washer must have a hole larger than the nut.

Conduit

Nut

Washers

Threaded rod

Coupling nut

Gravel bed

Through-bolts

Lag bolts

Freestanding lumber beds

When the soil is very rocky or you're building on a rooftop or terrace, you need a freestanding bed. Without stakes to bear the load, however, you must use cross ties to keep the sides from bowing out like a rowboat.

While 2x4 ties can be used, they are subject to terrific strain at their ends—enough in some cases to tear out the small amount of wood between a fastener and the end of the 2x4. Stronger and less conspicuous ties can be made with long rods that are threaded like bolts (see the drawing above). Whereas bolts employ a head on one end and a nut on the other end for tightening,

threaded rods employ two nuts—one on each end. Threaded rods are available in most lumberyards and hardware stores.

Pass the rod through a sleeve of metal electrical conduit to give it some protection from corrosion. The conduit will also lock in the precise width of the bed. Since threaded rods are most commonly sold in 3-ft. lengths, you may need more than one length to span your raised bed. In that case, splice the two rods with a coupling nut. Be sure your metal sleeve is large enough to admit the coupling nut as well as the rod itself. A nominal ¾-in. conduit accommodates a ⅜-in. rod with a coupling nut.

Log-cabin timber beds

Log-cabin beds are easy to build and are very durable. They can be constructed of square timbers or semisquare landscape timbers. Their one drawback is that the width of the timbers reduces the available soil space when compared to 2x lumber. On the other hand, having a wide edge on which to park your elbow or derriere while plucking weeds is not a bad idea.

To simplify cutting, make all of the side timbers equal and all of the end timbers equal (see the drawing at right). Predrill your timbers before assembly to make spiking easier. Preassemble the first two courses of each side on some hard surface and then connect them at the corners *in situ* (for more on building this type of bed, see the photo essay on p. 108). Long screws work best for these four initial corners because the assembly won't be solid enough at this point to withstand hammer blows without bouncing around. After the second

These raised beds are constructed of 4x6s with log-cabin corners. The heavy sides resist bowing out. (Builder: Peter Kreyling.)

LOG-CABIN CORNERS

To simplify cutting, make the length of the timbers the same in all courses.

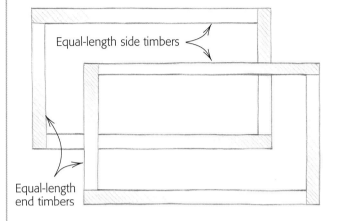

Equal-length side timbers

Equal-length end timbers

It will take longer to cut if you make the length of the timbers alternate from short to long between courses.

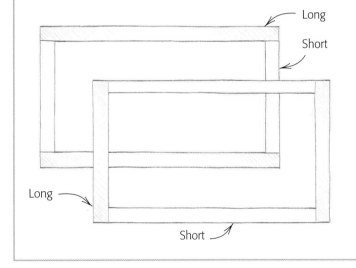

Long

Short

Long

Short

FREESTANDING LANDSCAPE TIMBER BED

Timbers are strong enough to resist soil pressure on their own.
Cross ties aren't needed unless the bed is more than 8 ft. long.

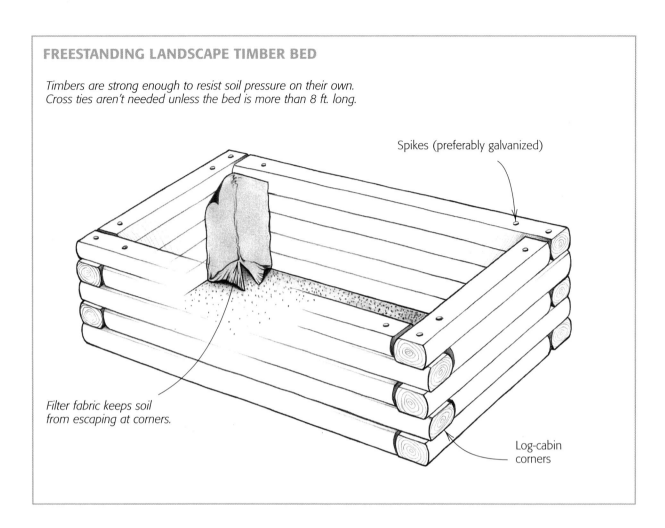

Spikes (preferably galvanized)

Filter fabric keeps soil
from escaping at corners.

Log-cabin
corners

course, you will be able to pound in spikes as fasteners.

When making log–cabin corners with semisquare landscape timbers, there will be gaps between the square end of each timber and the rounded side of the adjoining timber. To keep soil from leak–ing out through these gaps, staple filter fabric to the inside of the bed at the corners before filling the bed with soil (see the drawing above). To avoid gaps altogether, you can miter the corners of landscape–timber beds (see the top photo on the facing page). Use mending plates to reinforce the miter joint in every course.

LAYING OUT AND PREPARING THE SITE

A raised bed that will be placed on a patio or driveway has a ready–made foundation. It can be assembled on site, shoved into position, and filled. A raised bed on a deck or rooftop should be approached with caution, though. Wet soil weighs over 100 lb. per cubic foot. For a 4-ft. by 8-ft. bed, only 12 in. deep, that works out to more than $1\frac{1}{2}$ tons. Have an architect or engineer assess the structure's ability to carry such a load. If you live in an apartment building, notify the superintendent of your intentions.

Some site preparation is required if a bed will be placed on a lawn or meadow. Begin by laying out the bed's footprint with strings, powdered lime, or spray paint. Be sure to make the corners square. If you have a sheet of plywood on hand, you can ensure square corners for a bed 4 ft. wide by spray-painting around the sheet of plywood.

When the layout is complete, remove strips of turf 2 in. wider than the bed's sides and a couple inches deep. Outline the strips with a spade, then peel back the turf with a mattock, or use a fork or spade to cut out smaller squares. The remaining turf within the confines of the bed will rot when the bed is filled.

Where the turf was removed, cut shallow trenches level with the lowest corner (you can eyeball this). If you overdig in places, build the trench back up with gravel or compacted earth. If there's a substantial grade change from one end of the bed to the other, you may consider using narrower boards in the places where the grade is highest (see the bottom photo at right). There's no point in burying an entire side board below grade. When the trenches are level and fairly smooth all around, the "foundation" is complete.

Landscape timbers can be log-cabined together (back) or mitered (middle). Concealed metal plates reinforce the miters (front).

You can use a narrow board in the lower course (left) if the grade surrounding the bed is higher on one side.

FILLING THE BED

Before filling a raised bed, consider turning over and amending some of the native soil below the bed. As well as encouraging root growth and the local worm population, this brings certain trace minerals up out of the subsoil. These oft-overlooked nutrients are sometimes absent from topsoil. When spading, don't disturb the soil on which the sides rest.

When a raised bed sits on a hard surface such as a patio, you can improve drainage by putting down a 3-in. layer of small stones or gravel on the bottom of the bed before filling. Then add a layer of filter fabric to isolate gravel from soil. To allow water in the gravel bed to escape, shim up the sides of the bed with a few 20d galvanized spikes laid sideways on the patio. This produces a ¼-in. drainage gap all around the base of the bed.

A staked bed may look utilitarian, but it's the least expensive raised bed to build. The only difficulty that may arise is driving the stakes. (This bed shouldn't be used on rocky soils, where driving the stakes accurately is a problem, or on rooftops or patios.) Because stakes give the bed most of its support, you probably won't need a cross tie. However, if you're in doubt about the strength of the stakes, you can add a cross tie to be on the safe side (see the photo above).

Here, the stakes are placed on the outside of the bed so that soil pressure holds the side boards against the stakes. If you don't like that look, you can put the side boards outside the stakes, but you will need to fasten them with bolts instead of nails because soil pressure will be constantly pushing the boards away from the stakes. This look is similar to that of a freestanding bed, which requires a cross tie and doesn't use stakes (see the drawing on p. 102).

1 Line up and drive the stakes to support the sides of the bed. The tops of the stakes should all be level. Dig a shallow trench just inside the line of stakes.

2 Screw the top course of side boards to the inside of the stakes. Then screw the lower course of side boards up tight against the top course.

3 Screw the end boards to the stakes and use a metal strap to reinforce the connection.

4 You can add a 2x4 cross tie to intermediate stakes to keep the sides of the bed from spreading once it's filled.

If you want a rustic look for your garden, this is the raised bed for you. Landscape timbers lend a natural, Davy Crockett look to the structure, and they have more character than plain boards. For a more geometric look, you can use square timbers instead of round.

The construction of this type of bed is simplicity itself. There are no cross ties and no special fasteners—just big spikes. The only tools you'll need are a saw, a drill, and a hammer, and the intentionally rough look of this bed means you don't have to worry about making perfect cuts. Just be careful when you pick out your landscape timbers; because they are produced from young trees, they are often twisted and warped.

When you design the bed, try to minimize the number of cuts necessary, because uncut timbers last longer. In other words, if you buy 8-ft. lengths, make an 8-ft. by 4-ft. bed so you don't have to cut the side timbers, and you'll get exactly two end timbers per piece.

1 Using string and stakes or a plywood template as a guide, lay out the bed with powdered lime along the outside of the bed's footprint. Then outline the edges of the trench with a spade, and strip back the turf using a mattock. Add gravel to the trench and level it.

2 Spike together the first two courses for each side. Offset their ends by the width of a timber.

3 Overlap the first and second course subassemblies and screw them together.

4 Spike subsequent courses in place. A helper can apply some weight to hold the timber steady.

8 Arbors, Pergolas, and Trellises

The use of lightweight wooden skeletons to support climbing plants is as old as agriculture. Indeed, garden structures are suggested by the forest itself, where living trees provide an armature for sun-thirsty creepers. While the leafy finery that adorns an arbor, pergola, or trellis is the icing on the cake, the best examples possess beauty in their own right. These structures achieve their good looks by the artful arrangement of slender parts in regular patterns.

One hoped-for result of this arrangement is a lively sense of visual rhythm (see the photo at right). Another sought-after effect is symmetry. Both of these qualities are inherently pleasing to us as human beings, and they may acquire even greater drama when set against the asymmetry of nature (see the photo on the facing page). Considering the small investment of labor and material they require, arbors, pergolas, and trellises deliver more than just about any other home project. (Photo essays on building an arbor, a pergola with seats, and a trellis with a planter begin on p. 120.)

Because regular spacing plays such an important part in building skeletal structures, it's important to know how to mark, cut, and assemble groups of uniform parts efficiently, as well as how to raise the structures.

MARKING AND CUTTING PARTS

The first step in constructing a skeletal structure is to take a hard, analytical look at the design. Most garden support structures consist of a few basic parts,

The regular spacing of the roof poles on this arbor sets up a pleasing visual rhythm. (Designer: Florence Everts; builder: Peter Kreling.)

Compared to a circular saw, a jigsaw (or sabersaw) is versatile and safe. Its narrow blade cuts curves easily, and because it produces less friction, kickback is virtually eliminated. On the downside, a jigsaw cuts slower than a circular saw and doesn't produce as straight a cut.

The difference in performance between homeowner and professional models is especially noticeable in the jigsaw family. Professional models have an elliptical blade motion that cuts much more effi-ciently than the straight up-and-down motion of homeowner types. Professional jigsaws also have a guide bearing that supports the blade, giving better control. The projects illustrated in this book can be tackled with a homeowner-type jigsaw, but the job will take longer. Try out different models, and buy the best you can afford.

For landscape carpentry, a coarse-toothed blade is usually all you'll need. If you desire a smooth edge, switch to a fine-toothed blade or sand the edges.

produced in multiples and arranged in regular patterns. List each type of part on paper, along with the quantity and the exact size. Precut all the parts and stack them in neat piles.

Before marking or fastening anything together, try arranging the parts loosely into subassemblies. By doing so, you'll understand how the parts fit together and recognize any problems before you're in the middle of construction. For instance, to mock up the side panels for an arbor, lay two posts on the ground and spread a set of cross members across the posts in their approximate locations. Do the same for the roof assembly. An experienced builder may be able to skip over these preliminaries, but novices will have a much clearer idea of where they are headed after completing this exercise.

Once the general scheme of things has been rehearsed, it's time to mark the precise spacing of individual members.

The strong symmetry of this trellis extends right down to the clasped hands of the angel in the center. Swirling around this peaceful center is a raucous wisteria vine. (Designer/builder: Lawrence Dreschler.)

LAYING OUT POSTS FOR A PERGOLA

Lay out all four posts at the same time. Using the working drawing as a guide, make a layout stick with six key measurements. Transfer these measurements to the posts before cutting and assembly begins. A seventh measurement on the rod for grade is only approximate. The actual grade will vary.

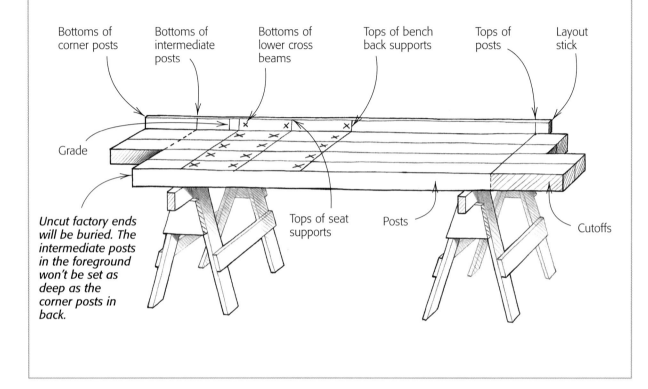

Bottoms of corner posts

Bottoms of intermediate posts

Bottoms of lower cross beams

Tops of bench back supports

Tops of posts

Layout stick

Grade

Uncut factory ends will be buried. The intermediate posts in the foreground won't be set as deep as the corner posts in back.

Tops of seat supports

Posts

Cutoffs

It's much quicker and more accurate to perform this marking simultaneously on groups of parts rather than marking each piece after it's been installed. If you want to prime your parts with paint, do so before penciling in the layout.

Begin the marking process with the main posts. Nestle a group of posts together side by side with their ends carefully lined up (see the drawing above). Then mark cross-member locations on one of the posts. (You can even wait until this point to mark the overall length of the posts rather than measuring each one individually.) Do your measuring with a tape measure, or pre-

pare a special layout stick with only the necessary measurements on it. As a way of working out details in advance, builders and cabinetmakers like to develop a complete set of layout sticks (one for height, one for breadth, and one for width) before a single piece of wood is cut.

After establishing cross-member locations on one of the posts, use a square to extend the marks onto all the posts in the group. You can mark where both edges of the cross member will go, but laying out just one edge is all that's really necessary. Just make sure you mark an X to show which side of the line the cross member will go on. After marking the posts, mark the other members as sets as well.

Before putting subassemblies together, perform any detail work that's required on the pieces, such as beveling or scroll cutting the ends. You can even sand and apply water repellent at this point to avoid climbing on a ladder later on.

When the parts are ready, lay out the structure's footprint and assemble the parts into as large a unit as you can comfortably erect. How big the unit is may depend on the number (and size) of your helpers. A small arbor might be fully assembled before installation, whereas a convenient subassembly for a pergola might consist of just two posts and a cross beam.

BUILDING WOODEN ARCHES

An important subassembly in many garden projects is the arch. A shallow arch can be cut from a single wide board (see the photo at right). A deep arch can be cut from a sheet of plywood, but plywood doesn't hold up well outdoors, especially with its edges exposed. A better solution for a deep arch is to join several pieces of solid lumber together by using a technique called bricklaying. In bricklaying, individual curved segments are stacked with their ends staggered to create an overlap–sort of like laying bricks (see the drawing above).

To make templates for the overlapping arch segments, first lay out the arch full scale on a sheet of ¼-in. plywood, then divide it into thirds. A large arch may need to be divided into more than three segments, whereas a small arch might be built up from just two. The wider the boards you have to work with, the fewer segments will be required.

COMPOSING A BIRCH-LAID ARCH

Each arch requires two outer layers and one middle layer. Total pieces required for job: 16 segment pieces and 4 dogleg pieces. (Each arbor requires two arches.)

Outside layers consist of three segment pieces each

Middle layer consists of two segment pieces and two dogleg pieces

Dogleg piece has straight section to act as tenon

The shallow arches of this arbor were sawn from wide redwood boards.

The chopsaw and table saw are two semiportable tools that could come in handy for building some of the projects in this book. For general carpentry work, the chopsaw is especially valuable. In addition to trim, it cuts 2x4s and 2x6s with speed and precision. And by turning a board around, you can even cut wider stock. The chopsaw can be mounted on a stand, but for working around the yard, it's simpler just to plop it on the ground. To support long boards during a cut, slip a couple of blocks under the end of the board. For safety, don't cut anything less than 6 in. long. If you need a 4-in. piece, for instance, cut it off the end of a longer board.

When shopping for a chopsaw, pay special attention to weight. The lighter the machine, the more useful it will be. There are several good models out there weighing just 28 lb.

Another semiportable tool that's very handy is the compact table saw. Its primary purpose is ripping (cutting with the grain), and it cuts thin strips easily. You can buy a metal stand for the saw, but attaching it to a pair of low sawhorses works just as well.

One of the dangers of using a table saw is kickback. This can occur when friction

A motorized chopsaw makes short work of cutting both lumber and trim. Miter cuts, like the one shown here, are as easy as square cuts.

develops between the blade and the workpiece, causing the workpiece to be thrown back toward the operator. Kickback can be caused by accidentally wiggling the workpiece or by a sudden warping of the workpiece as tensions

A portable table saw is ideal for ripping wide boards into narrow ones. Set the height of the blade so that it protrudes just slightly above the workpiece—about the height of a tooth. (The guard has been removed for clarity.)

boards freehand (without a fence) because even a slight wiggling of the board may cause a kickback.

The worst table-saw accidents occur when the operator reaches behind the blade to control or retrieve a workpiece. If the workpiece accidentally kicks back at this point, it may drag a hand with it. Just as dangerous is the possibility of a loose sleeve or bracelet catching on the blade. For these reasons, always use a push stick to guide the work past the cut, and have a helper support the work as it exits from the saw so you don't have to reach behind the blade. And whenever you work with a table saw, remove any loose jewelry and button your shirt cuffs or roll up your sleeves to the elbow.

As with a chopsaw, weight is the primary consideration when buying a portable table saw. Aside from being light, a small table saw is easy to stash under a workbench or in a closet. Another important feature of any table saw is the rip fence. It should be easy to adjust, and it should stay parallel with the blade without any fussing. A nonparallel rip fence is another potential source of kickback.

within the board are released by cutting. To reduce the likelihood of kickback, adjust the blade so that it just clears the work, thereby reducing friction. Never rip

LAYING OUT ARCH SEGMENTS
WITH A TRAMMEL STICK

Step 1
Set the nail in the trammel stick at A (center of arch). Use pencil holes 1 and 2 (outside and inside radii) to draw the arch.

1

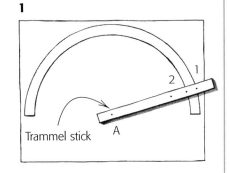

Trammel stick · A

Step 2
Set the center nail at B on the outside circumference. Use the line made by pencil hole 1 (outside radius) to divide the outside circumference into ⅓ segment, crossing the circumference at C. Repeat on the other side, with center 1 at D and crossing at E.

2 & 3

C · E · B · A · D

Step 3
Connect C and E to center point A, thus dividing the arch into three equal segments.

4, 5 & 6

Step 4
Using D and E as center points and an arbitrary distance as a radius (pencil hole 3), swing overlapping arcs.

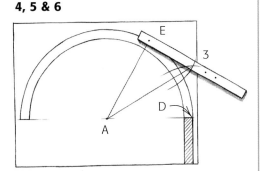

E · 3 · D · A

Step 5
Connect the center of arch A to the point where arcs overlap, thus dividing a ⅓ segment into two ⅙ segments.

Step 6
Extend the arch with straight lines to form a tenon.

To lay out the curve of the arch, use a trammel stick—a sort of overgrown compass (see the center right photo on p. 121). A nail protrudes through the stick at one end to act as a center point, while the other end has holes drilled at different locations to receive a pencil.

You can also use the trammel stick to divide the arch into segments (see the drawings at left). The basic geometry is: When the radius of a circle is "stepped off" along the circle's circumference three times, the distance traveled will equal one half of the circle, or the arch.

After laying out and dividing the arch on plywood, cut the segments out and use them as templates. In addition to one-third segments, one-sixth segments will be required at both ends of the arch to create an offset in one of the layers, in the same way that a half brick is used in every other course of a brick wall. In the example shown in the drawing on the facing page, a straight section has been added to the one-sixth segment to form a tenon that will interlock with the post of the arbor.

Place the templates on the workpieces and trace them. Then cut out the pieces with a jigsaw or bandsaw. To assemble the arch, start by layering a one-sixth segment onto a one-third segment, keeping the edges carefully aligned. Add another one-third segment next, and so on, until the arch is complete. The process is sort of like leap-frogging. A combination of glue and screws works well for laminating the pieces.

Arch segments are prone to splitting because their grain runs diagonally across the segment at each end, a condition known as short grain. To keep the short grain from splitting, be sure to drill pilot holes for nails or screws.

Straight 1x4s layered together to make posts

Tenon added to ⅙ segment of arch to interlock with post

Edge view of arch

LEVELING POST HOLES

After putting together the assembly (or subassemblies), check the as–built distance between posts against the footprint layout you did on the ground. If the measurements check out, go ahead and dig your holes. If not, adjust the footprint accordingly.

The bottoms of your post holes must be level with each other or the structure will not stand straight. The question is how to gauge the depth of the holes in relation to each other, since a spirit level can't be placed directly between the bottoms of the holes. Knowing the depth of the holes below grade isn't much help because the grade itself is almost always out of level. So to check for level, builders use an optical instrument with a telescope and a special calibrated rod.

Fortunately, most garden structures are compact, which allows you to use a simple method for gauging the depth of post holes. Start by setting a stake somewhere in the middle of the footprint as an arbitrary benchmark (see the drawing on p. 118). Drive the stake with a sledgehammer until it feels good and solid. If the top of the stake slopes much in any direction, saw it off to produce a fairly level surface.

Now find a straightedge long enough to reach horizontally from the stake to each hole (a straight 2x4 will do nicely). Tape your spirit level to the straightedge. (If your level is long enough by itself, you won't need the straightedge.)

Rest one end of the straightedge on the stake, and hold the other end against a folding rule or tape measure held vertically in the hole. Move the free end of the straightedge up or down until the bubble in the level reads true, and then see where the top of the straightedge crosses the ruler. Write down the measurement. Now do the same thing with the other post holes and compare the measurements.

Add a few inches of gravel to each hole for drainage, adding somewhat more to the deepest holes and somewhat less to the shallower holes. Check the measurements again, and adjust the depths with more gravel as necessary. Don't go crazy. If you get all the measurements within ½ in., you're okay. After raising the structure into position, you can fine-tune the alignment by beating on the tops of too–high posts with a sledgehammer (be sure to use a block of wood as a cushion to prevent damage to the post).

The top of a stake serves as an arbitrary benchmark. By measuring the depth of each hole in relation to the stake, the bottoms of the holes can be leveled with each other.

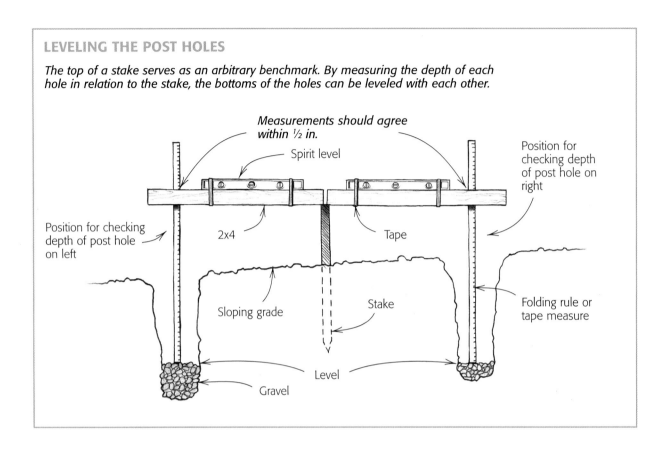

Measurements should agree within ½ in.

Spirit level

Position for checking depth of post hole on right

Position for checking depth of post hole on left

2x4

Tape

Sloping grade

Stake

Folding rule or tape measure

Gravel

Level

TYING, BRACING, AND BACKFILLING

A large structure such as a pergola is best raised in two half sections, with each section consisting of two posts and a primary cross member (see the top drawing on the facing page). After raising both half sections, tie them together with secondary cross members going perpendicular to the primary cross members. For instance, the pergola shown on p. 124 is built with rafters (roof beams) acting as primary cross members. After the pergola's post-and-rafter subassemblies were raised into position, they were tied together by headers (load-bearing horizontal beams). All sorts of cross-member arrangements are possible, which can make carpentry

nomenclature rather subjective. The underlying idea, however, is that one set of cross members supports a second set oriented perpendicular to the first.

When both sets of cross members are in place, the overall dimensions of the structure will be locked in at the tops of the posts, but the bottoms are still free to move around. Solve this by tacking temporary horizontal battens just above grade to hold the bottoms of the posts the correct distance apart during back-filling (see the middle drawing on the facing page). Before installing the battens, mark on each end the correct post-to-post distance. (This distance can be read off the plans or simply transferred from the top of the assembly, where the posts are already joined together by cross members.)

When the bottoms of the posts are held together properly, the posts will all be parallel, but they may still be out of plumb. This effect is called racking. To ensure that the posts remain truly plumb (vertical) while the backfilling is completed, the structure must be braced diagonally (see the bottom drawing at right). First, drive stakes in the ground a few feet from each corner. Then nail a temporary diagonal brace from each stake to the top of its corresponding post to stiffen the structure and hold it plumb. You'll need to gauge the plumb-ness of the post with a level as you nail the brace. If it's out of plumb, have a helper lean on the post as you drive a nail through the brace into the post.

Now backfill all the holes (for more on backfilling posts, see Chapter 9). Once all the holes have been backfilled, remove the diagonal braces and tempo-rary horizontal battens—the earth will hold the posts upright.

COMPLETING THE SKELETON

Once the basic framework of a structure has been erected, additional parts are usually added as infill. These parts can be attached in different ways.

Notching is a positive and attractive way to connect heavy timbers, but it may weaken lighter boards. It can also cause short sections of wood beyond the notch to split off.

Instead of notching parts, nail them to each other, being sure to mark them with the correct spacing beforehand. A part may bow inward or outward, but lining it up with the correct marks on the adjoining part will straighten it. Some persuasion may be necessary. Press on the offending part with a hand or foot as the adjoining part is being nailed on, or pry it into position.

TYING AND BRACING POSTS

Step 1
When the half sections are raised, the posts are nonparallel and out of plumb.

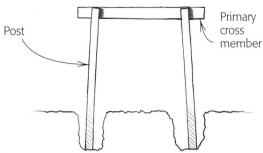

Post

Primary cross member

Step 2
Tack a temporary horizontal batten in place just above grade so that the posts are parallel, although they may still be out of plumb (racked).

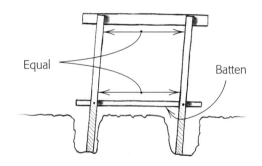

Equal

Batten

Step 3
Then attach diagonal braces to the structure to ensure that the posts are parallel and plumb—ready for backfill.

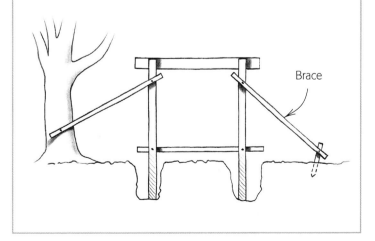

Brace

his arched arbor is a classic. Of course, the arch makes this one of the more challenging projects in the book. If you take it one step at a time, however, it will be manageable. The geometry of the circle is actually fairly simple, which makes this circular arch a lot less troublesome than elliptical versions. If you're nervous about the arch, you can do a square-top arbor instead. The look would be similar to the top of a basic pergola.

The arch and posts of this arbor are built up by layering thin boards together, which simplifies the joinery. For instance, by extending the middle layer of the arch, a tenon is produced so you don't have to saw this joint separately from a thick piece (see the drawing on p. 117). Portions of the middle layer have been left out of the posts to give the structure an airy feeling.

For a more opaque arbor, you can add vertical as well as horizontal battens to the sides or attach prefab lattice panels. To increase the diameter of the arch, you'll need wider boards and perhaps a greater number of segments making up the curve. When upsizing, you might also consider using three layers of 5/4 lumber instead of the 1x shown here to maintain the proper scale.

1 Rack up 1x4s for posts side by side for marking, along with filler blocks. Use a framing square to mark all the pieces at once.

2 To make each post, assemble a pair of 1x4s with blocks in between. The open space left between the blocks gives the arbor a light appearance. The letter B written on the outer layers indicates the location of a block.

3 Lay out the arch on a sheet of plywood, using a trammel stick to draw the inner and outer curves (see the drawings on p. 116).

4 Trace the dogleg template onto a blank of cedar and mark the spring line for the arch. The spring line is where the end of the first segment piece will be positioned when the lamination process begins. Cut out the piece with a jigsaw.

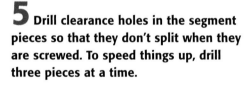

5 Drill clearance holes in the segment pieces so that they don't split when they are screwed. To speed things up, drill three pieces at a time.

6 Laminate the segment pieces together using galvanized screws and waterproof glue.

7 Attach the arch to the post by slipping the straight portion of the dogleg piece between 1x4s.

8 Set the arch/post assembly in the post holes.

9 After marking the post locations on the crosspieces, screw them to the posts.

10 Plumb the posts, then install some temporary bracing. After bracing the arbor, backfill the post holes.

11 Attach additional cross beams at the arch.

This pergola with seats and lattice panels is a nice variation of the basic form. The seats add a functional aspect, as does the lattice, which vines can easily grow on. If you don't want lattice, consider providing some sort of ladder to assist small vines as they grow up the posts. This can be wire netting, strings, or a series of nails or dowels set partway into the posts.

The "roof" of a pergola can be a simple set of rafters going in one direction, or you can add purlins at right angles to the rafters to produce the crisscross pattern shown here. Curved details like the scalloped seat slats and the scrolled ends of the rafters give the pergola a graceful look. These cuts are easy to make with a jigsaw. If you don't have a jigsaw, you can still produce decorative effects by pointing or beveling the various members with straight cuts. For instance, the lower corner of each rafter can be chopped off at a 45° angle instead of scroll cutting.

For a more traditional and open pergola, you could omit the lattice panels and the seats. In that case you won't need the intermediate posts either—just the four corner posts.

1 Lay out the structure's footprint with stringlines or a plywood template. Then simulate the location of a 4x4 post relative to the footprint by placing a 4x4 block just inside the layout lines. Spray paint around the block to lay out the surrounding post hole. Once the holes are marked, you can dig them.

2 After crosscutting the rafters to length, trim their ends with a jigsaw. Use a plywood template to outline this decorative cut.

3 Line up the rafters side by side, then lay out the purlin locations on the rafters' top edges.

4 Mark header locations (left) on the undersides of the two intermediate rafters. Mark post locations (right) on the undersides of the two outer rafters.

5 Cut the 4x4 posts to length (see the drawing on p. 112), then screw each outside rafter to a pair of posts.

6 Raise the first post/rafter assembly into position. Once this one is up, you can raise the next one.

7 Install a header to tie the two post/rafter assemblies together at the top. Then install a seat ledger to tie the two post/rafter assemblies together at the bottom.

8 Tack temporary battens on the long sides to hold the bottoms of the posts the correct distance apart, then install temporary diagonal bracing to hold the structure plumb. After the bracing is installed, backfill and tamp the holes.

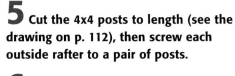

9 Attach intermediate posts against the outside rafters with screws, then install permanent corner braces for extra rigidity.

10 Nail diagonal lattice panels onto the framing.

11 Toenail intermediate rafters onto the headers, lay out the rafter locations on the purlins, then nail the purlins onto the rafters. Crooked rafters may have to be pushed into position to line up correctly with the marks on the purlins.

12 Make the back of the seat with decorative slats.

This trellis with a planter is attractive, freestanding, and moveable. It's easy to build, and you can modify the design to suit your needs. For instance, you can downsize the planter to produce a window box, or you can build the trellis by itself to put up against your house. Cutouts in the latticework can produce interesting "windows" for vines to grow around. To impart a rustic look, use saplings for the trellis instead of lumber. Coping and molding around the edge of the planter give it a finished look, but they might be out of place on a naturalized version.

To simplify the jobs of marking and cutting, lay out all the trellis parts at once. Standard 1x boards are fine for the trellis, but you'll need thicker boards to hold the earth in place in the planter. This planter is made with 5/4 boards, but a wider 4-ft. version would require 2x lumber for strength.

Notice that the grain on the planter's end boards runs vertically. This is important because screws driven into the edge of a board will hold securely; screws driven into end grain will not. If the end boards were positioned horizontally, the screws holding the front and back would be going into end grain. Eventually, the screws would pull out (for more on end grain vs. side grain, see p. 18).

1 Predrill the side boards to avoid splitting them when they are screwed. Drilling three at once saves time.

2 Trim away part of the lowermost side board, leaving a short, uncut section at both ends. This forms little legs at the four corners to keep the planter from tipping and to promote drainage.

3 Screw the side boards to the 2x12 end boards.

4 Nail the 2x12 bottom board in place, then drill drainage holes in it.

5 Rip the 2½-in.-wide copings on a table saw and miter the ends with a hand miter box or a chopsaw. You can also cut the miter joint with a circular saw, retracting the blade guard with your thumb to keep it from binding. Retracting the blade guard isn't necessary with square cuts.

6 Nail the copings to the top edges of the planter. Keep the miter joint aligned with a C-clamp, then use finish nails to fasten the joint permanently.

7 Miter one end of a molding, then hold the piece in position and mark the other end.

8 Cut the miter joint on a hand miter box or with a chopsaw.

9 Mark the trellis' vertical pieces to show the locations of the horizontal pieces. Use a bar clamp to hold the pieces in alignment for marking. Mark the horizontals in the same way to show the location of the verticals.

10 Transfer layout marks from one of the horizontal pieces to the back of the planter.

11 Screw vertical pieces for the trellis to the back of the planter.

12 Fasten the cross pieces to the vertical pieces with finish nails. Then drive screws in from the back to reinforce the overlaps.

9

Fences

Wooden fence styles run the gamut from crude to refined, with every imaginable variant in between. Choosing a fence for your yard means finding a style that is both functional and visually harmonious with its surroundings. For instance, a Federal-style fence in front of a log cabin would be as incongruous as a split-rail fence aound a townhouse.

Beyond taste, there are practical questions to be answered before you can choose the right fence. For most of us, cost will be a controlling factor, but how difficult the fence is to install is also important. Different fences require different levels of skill to build, as well as different tools. If you already have woodworking skills and an arsenal of power tools, you may opt to build an elaborate fence from scratch. If you feel comfortable with rough carpentry but not finish work, you may stick with a simple fence or buy a fancy prefabricated panel that you can apply to your own rough substructure.

Time is another consideration. A fence can be a big project. If time is abundant and money is short, you'll probably want to tackle every phase of the project yourself. But if 9 o'clock tennis sounds better than digging post holes or brushing on stain, you may want to farm out part or all of the work to a contractor or build a simpler fence. Consider the time required for future maintenance as well. In general, the more rustic the style, the less upkeep it will need.

TYPES OF FENCES

Wood fences can be divided into two broad categories: open fences and screening fences. In more rural areas, open fences are used to delineate broad areas of landscape, but they're also used in suburban settings where privacy is not a concern. Screening fences are typically found in close proximity to homes. They provide privacy between neighbors and block out unsightly views.

Open fences

The two main types of open, or see-through, fences are board fences and post-and-rail fences. The difference lies mainly in their horizontal members.

Board fencing graces the pasture along this rural roadside.

Board fences employ flat boards, whereas post–and–rail fences use chunkier members, such as round poles or square timbers.

Board fences Board fencing is a standard feature of the American landscape (see the photo above). In its simplest form, it consists of posts on 8–ft. centers, with three or four 1x6 rails (horizontal boards) nailed on one side. However, this basic theme can be varied in a number of ways.

Posts for this type of fence are usually roughsawn 4x4s. Round posts can be used, but they won't provide good bearing for the boards (see the drawings at right). To compensate for this, you can cut shallow notches into the posts or try a half-round post. The flat side of the

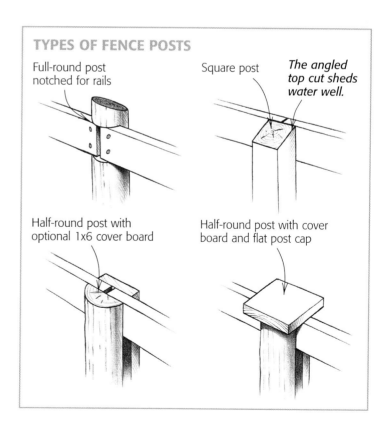

TYPES OF FENCE POSTS

Full-round post notched for rails

Square post

The angled top cut sheds water well.

Half-round post with optional 1x6 cover board

Half-round post with cover board and flat post cap

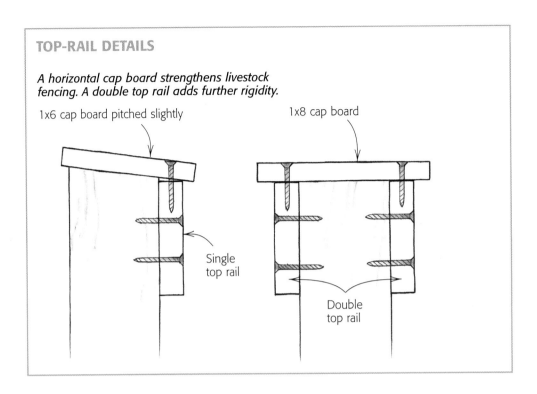

TOP-RAIL DETAILS

A horizontal cap board strengthens livestock fencing. A double top rail adds further rigidity.

1x6 cap board pitched slightly

1x8 cap board

Single top rail

Double top rail

A board fence with cross-buck rails strays from the ordinary.

half-round post provides a good nailing surface, while the round side has a more natural look to it than a square post. Half-round posts also cost less than square. Nailing a vertical 1x6 cover board on top of a half-round post dresses up the fence and gives the post more visual weight.

Rails are produced in pressure-treated (PT) yellow pine and unseasoned oak. The PT product has greater decay resistance, but the oak has much greater strength. Rails are typically roughsawn, measuring a full 1 in. by 6 in. by 16 ft. long. To strengthen the fence, stagger the joints between rails so they don't all fall on a single post. To strengthen the top rail, nail a flat cover board to its edge to create a member with an L cross section (see the drawing above). Combining the cover board with an additional rail on

To accommodate changes in a fence's direction, posts are drilled in a variety of ways.

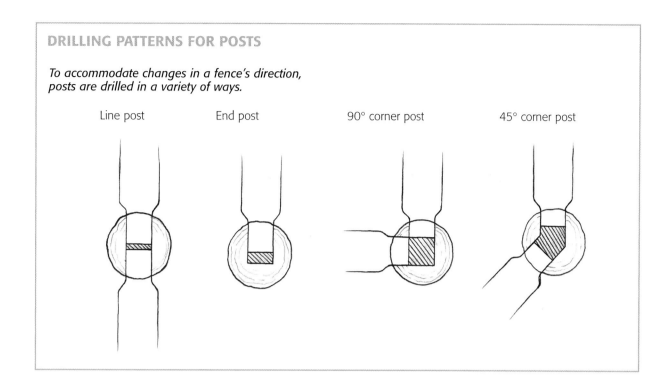

Line post   End post   90° corner post   45° corner post

the other side of the post will make an even stronger U-shaped assembly.

Although rails usually run horizon-tally, a handsome board fence can be achieved with a cross-buck pattern (see the photo on the facing page). Or the spacing between horizontal boards can be varied to produce different effects.

Post-and-rail fences The post-and-rail fence is a cousin of the board fence. In this type of fence, the rail fits into a recess in the post instead of being nailed on. Posts are usually round, with circular or oblong holes to receive the rails. To allow a fence to change directions, posts are drilled in a variety of ways (see the drawings above). Prepare a list of the different types of posts you need before you talk to your fence supplier.

The rails are either full round or quarter round and may have either a dowel end for round holes or a scarfed

A square-cornered post-and-rail fence creates a geometric look.

A rustic picket fence of roughsawn oak creates a unique, natural look. Square-topped pickets alternate with spear points.

Narrow 1x1 pickets create a formal look on this village fence.

end for oblong holes. Square-cornered post-and-rail systems are also available for a more geometric look (see the photo on p. 135).

Screening fences

Screening fences can be used for privacy or to obscure unsavory items such as trash cans. Most screening fences consist of three elements: vertical posts, horizontal rails, and vertical pickets, or pales.

There are many versions of this type of fence. Posts can be partially or completely covered over on one side by the pickets, or they may be exposed on both sides if rails run between the posts. It's the pickets, though, that establish a

fence's identity through their color, texture, size, shape, and spacing. You can buy prefabricated fence panels or build your own fence on site from scratch.

Picket fences A picket fence, which is typically 2 ft. to 3 ft. tall, is often employed around a yard or garden. Posts are typically 4x4, 6 ft. to 8 ft. on center, and the rails are 2x4. The pickets are usually 1x3 or 1x4, with the tops cut in a decorative pattern. Narrow 1x1 pickets can also be used—closely spaced, they impart an aristocratic air (see the left photo above). You can buy prefabricated panels for a picket fence. But I've found that the panels often leave too much space between the pickets, so consider building your own (see p. 149 for a photo essay on building a picket fence).

One of the chief delights of the picket fence is the variety of ways in which the pickets can be arranged. Although a straight horizontal line across the top is common, there are many alternatives that can enliven the end product without substantially increasing its cost. For country gardens, rustic picket fences made of sticks and branches look great.

Because of the irregularity of the sticks, nailing can be difficult, but you can use galvanized wire lashing wrapped tightly around your sticks instead of nails. The use of roughsawn lumber can also lend a rustic air to a picket fence (see the right photo on the facing page).

Vertical-board fences A vertical-board fence provides maximum privacy. It is usually 6 ft. tall, with three 2x4 or 2x6 rails between posts. The posts are set 7 ft. or 8 ft. on center. You can buy pre-fabricated panels or assemble this type of fence piece by piece.

If you're using prefabricated panels, and you want the panels' rails to be the sole support for the pickets, you must place the posts very carefully so that the panels join directly over the centerline of each post (see the drawings at right); otherwise, you may have a partial picket or a gap where the panels join. To per-mit greater flexibility in the spacing of the posts, build a substructure of posts and subrails and then hang the panels consecutively on this substructure, regardless of the post placement. In this system, the rail that comes with the panel serves merely to hold the pickets together. To attach the panel to the sub-structure, nail through every fifth or sixth picket.

If you opt to build the panels your-self, the pickets—which are usually 1x6—can be applied in a variety of ways (see the drawings on p. 138). The tops can be trimmed in any style you like (for more on making pickets, see the sidebar on p. 141). For a finished appearance on both sides of the fence, apply pickets to both sides. Two sets of pickets double the weight on the rails, so either increase the size of the rails or build diagonal braces into the sub-structure. The braces have a truss effect

(see the drawings on p. 138)
see the sidebar on p. 141

PREFABRICATED FENCE PANELS

Prefabricated vertical-board fence panels can be mounted directly on posts, but the spacing of the posts must then be close to perfect. To accommodate irregular post spac-ing, attach subrails to the posts first. The panels can then hang on the subrails, independent of the posts.

Panels over posts (no subrails)

Joints between panels must occur at posts.

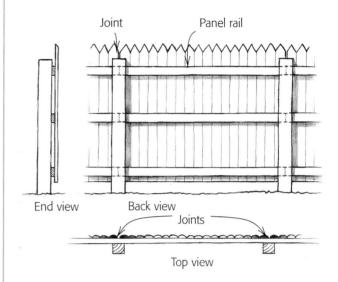

Joint   Panel rail

End view   Back view

Joints

Top view

Panels hang on subrails

Joints between panels can occur between posts.

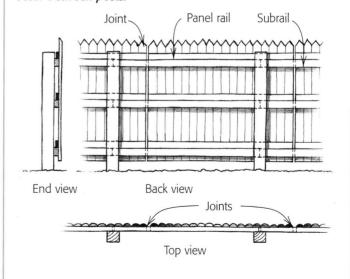

Joint   Panel rail   Subrail

End view   Back view

Joints

Top view

ATTACHING PICKETS

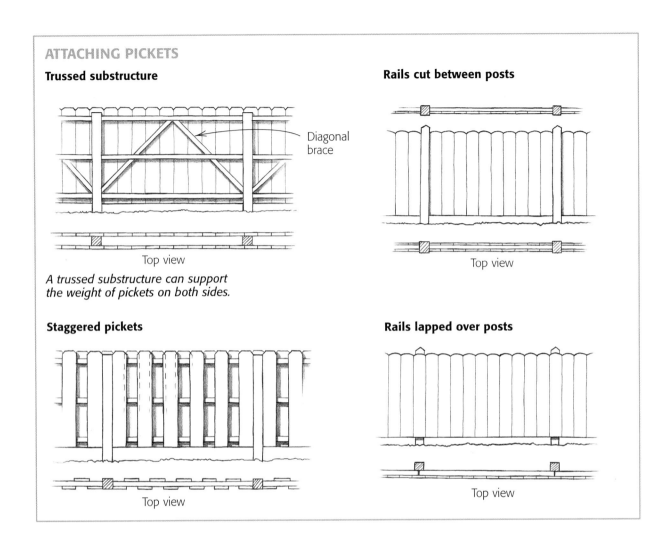

Trussed substructure

Diagonal brace

Top view

A trussed substructure can support the weight of pickets on both sides.

Rails cut between posts

Top view

Staggered pickets

Top view

Rails lapped over posts

Top view

This privacy fence has staggered pickets on both sides. A lattice "topper" extends the height of the fence without being overbearing.

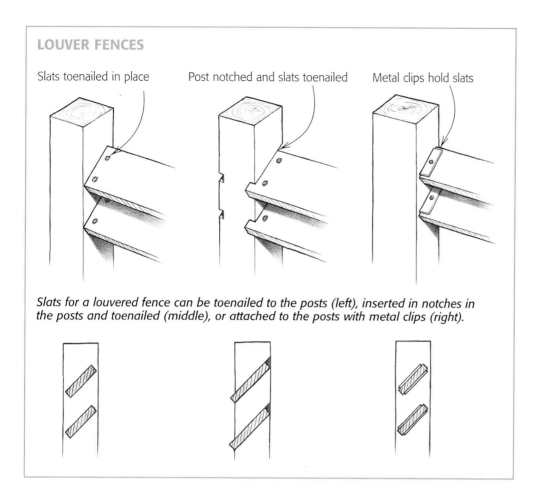

LOUVER FENCES

Slats toenailed in place

Post notched and slats toenailed

Metal clips hold slats

Slats for a louvered fence can be toenailed to the posts (left), inserted in notches in the posts and toenailed (middle), or attached to the posts with metal clips (right).

that keeps the rails from sagging. To create a same–on–both–sides fence without the extra weight and expense of double pickets, you can stagger a single set of pickets (see the photo on the facing page).

Stockade fences A stockade fence draws its inspiration from the palisade forts built on the American frontier. It is sold in panel form only. The pickets for this type of fence are tightly spaced half–round poles, about 3 in. in diameter, with pointed tops. Balsam fir is a popular species, as are spruce and cedar. The bark, which peels off eventually, is sometimes left on for an especially rustic look.

Louver fences A louver fence is made for privacy, with horizontal slats arranged on a downward slant, and has a breezy, contemporary look. You can mill grooves in the posts to receive the slats; simply toenail the slats in place, or use a metal clip to hold the slats (see the drawings above).

The posts for this type of fence shouldn't be too far apart, or the slats will sag. If you choose 1x4 or 1x6 slats, the maximum spacing would be about 6 ft. For 2x4 or 2x6 slats, you can increase the spacing to 10 ft.

Panel fences A panel fence is typically prefabricated and is available in many

This lattice-panel fence conceals a propane tank.

forms. For complete privacy, you can get panels consisting of solid boards laid tightly together within a frame. Another type has thin bands of wood woven closely together like a basket. The most common prefabricated panel is lattice, which offers partial screening without the heavy look of a solid fence (see the photo above).

Lattice panels are available in ½-in. and 1-in. thicknesses, which refer to the combined thickness of the overlapping battens. For example, ½-in. lattice has ¼-in.-thick battens, and 1-in. lattice has ½-in.-thick battens. The heavy material works best because it's strong and because the staples holding the lattice strips together have more to bite into. Premium lattice stock also has rounded corners.

Wood lattice is available in PT yellow pine and cedar. For low maintenance, vinyl lattice is also available. You can apply lattice diagonally, for a diamond pattern, or horizontally, in a tic-tac-toe motif.

To hold lattice panels in place, use 2x2 channel stock, which has a wide groove that engages the edge of the lattice. The channel stock can be fastened to rails and posts. The same effect can be achieved by nailing 1x1 stops on both sides of the panel.

Lattice panels are sold in 4x8 sheets. To create a 6–ft.–high fence, you can span the open space below the panel with closely spaced 1x4s or plant shrubbery. Trimming the top of a solid panel with a band of lattice (called a topper) produces a graceful look with full screening where it's needed most.

FENCE CONSTRUCTION

Once you've chosen the style of your fence, it's time to get down to work. First you'll need to lay out the fence line. The sweatiest part of the job will be digging holes for all the posts (for more information on digging post holes, see Chapter 4), and then setting and trimming them. Now the carpentry begins. You'll need to install horizontal boards or rails at the very least. When building a screening fence, you'll also be attaching vertical pickets to the rails

Making Fence Pickets

You can buy off-the-shelf fence pickets in a few basic patterns, but you can make much more interesting ones. To find a pattern you like, search the architecture section of your library. If you live near a town with fine old homes, take a walking tour. Better yet, design something yourself.

If you're cutting out individual pickets with a handsaw or a portable power saw, make a pattern from picket stock or something lighter, such as ¼-in. plywood. Trace the pattern onto each piece to guide the cut.

Radial-arm saws and chopsaws are effective for mass-producing simple, pointed pickets. To avoid having to measure each piece, set up a stop block, which is a block of wood nailed or clamped to the workbench a set distance from the saw-blade. By snugging the end of the picket stock against this block, you can cut each picket the same length. Also, by angling the sawblade, you can cut the pointy end of the picket without doing any layout. A single angle cut makes a sawtooth picket, while flipping the piece for a second cut produces a spear-tipped picket. To make a square 1x1 picket with a pyramid tip, rotate the piece four times.

Instead of precutting pickets, you may want to install oversize pickets, then trim their tops in place. A jigsaw works well for this, but you should try this technique only if you feel comfortable using a jigsaw in a vertical position. If the tops of the pickets are to line up in a straight line, install the oversize pickets and then snap a horizontal chalkline at the desired height. Trace the pattern onto each picket in accor-

Pickets can be cut with a jigsaw after they're installed.

dance with the chalkline, and cut them out (see the top photo above).

You can also trim the pickets along a curve, again using a jigsaw. Set nails at the high points of the curve, letting them stick out about 1 in. Then flex a thin wood batten into position between the nails and trace a line along the batten (see the bottom photo above). Cut directly along this curve or hold a pattern to each picket so that the points of the pickets align along the curve.

Use a thin batten to trace a curved line on the row of pickets. Then trim the pickets in place with a jigsaw.

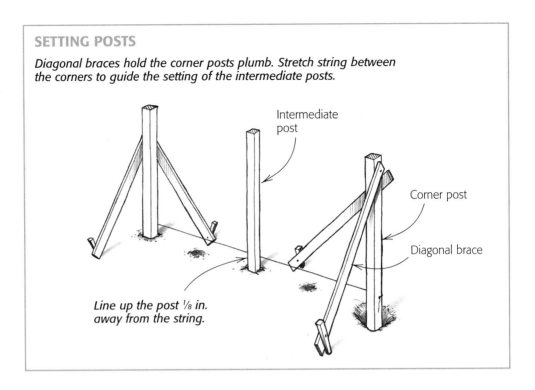

SETTING POSTS

Diagonal braces hold the corner posts plumb. Stretch string between the corners to guide the setting of the intermediate posts.

Intermediate post

Corner post

Diagonal brace

Line up the post ⅛ in. away from the string.

or hanging prefabricated panels be-tween the posts.

Laying out the fence line

To lay out the fence line, first locate its ends, along with any corners or changes in the fence's direction. Drive a stake at each location, then tie string between the stakes. When building a fence along the edge of your property, it's a good idea to hire a surveyor to locate your exact boundaries. Surveying is expen-sive, however, so you may decide to agree with your neighbor on a bound-ary instead. Consider, though, the possi-bility that you could both be mistaken. If either of you decides to sell, and a survey is made, difficulties could ensue.

Once the fence line is established, mark the location of intermediate posts. Maximum spacing will depend on the strength of the rails you're using. Adjust the spacing of the posts so that you don't have a short oddball section left over at the end of a run. The exception is a fence made of prefabricated panels, which may be difficult to adjust in width. When building a panel fence, it may be best to coordinate the post spacing carefully with the panels, even if that means relocating the ends or cor-ners of the fence.

Installing posts

Once you've marked the post locations, dig the post holes and begin setting the posts. Start with the corner posts. Plumb them with a spirit level, and brace them in two directions to hold them during backfilling. Tack the braces near the top of the fence post at one end and nail them to a tree or to a stake in the ground at the other end. Now pull a string between the corner posts to

Shaping Post Caps

Post caps can be as simple as a block of 2x6 nailed to a 4x4 post, but with a little extra fuss, you can produce shaped post caps that look better and last longer.

Post caps can be profiled in different ways. You can work a simple bevel on the cap with a block plane (see the photo at right). You can also cut corner bevels on a table saw, with the blade tilted to 45°. If you have a router, you can mold the edges of the post cap. To hold the cap securely while you rout the edges, temporarily tack the cap to a heavy plank with brads. Make sure the brads are placed far enough from the edge to avoid hitting them with the router bit.

A popular post-cap shape is a low pyramid, often with a finial at the top. The practical advantage of this design is that it sheds water faster than a flat post cap does. To produce the pyramid shape, tilt the blade of your table saw about 5°. You will be running the square post cap past the blade on edge (see the photo at right). To steady the work, fasten a high auxiliary fence to your table saw's regular fence. (The regular fence should have holes, allowing you to screw through the regular fence into the auxiliary fence.) Guide the post cap past the blade, pushing with one hand while using a push stick in the other to press the work against the fence.

A post cap can be beveled with a block plane.

You can saw a pyramid-shaped post cap on a table saw. Just be sure to use a push stick to keep your hand away from the blade.

To point the end of a post, make a bevel cut on each side.

guide the setting of the intermediate posts (see the drawing on p. 142). Set each intermediate post about ⅛ in. away from the string, with its face parallel with the string. Don't let the intermediate posts touch the string, or error will begin to accumulate. Plumb each post as its hole is backfilled. Don't worry if the tops of the posts don't line up at this point. They'll be trimmed evenly in the next step.

Trimming posts

After backfilling, trim the posts to a uniform height, which will make the fence run parallel to grade. Trimming the posts after they're installed is easier than trying to set all of them to the same height in the first place. Measure the height of each post above grade. Using the shortest post as the standard, cut off all the posts at the same height with a

small chainsaw or a handsaw. Cut the tops at a slight angle (about 10°) so that they'll shed water quicker (see the drawing on p. 133). An even more effective way to protect the top of a post is to nail on a short piece of board as a sloping lid or attach a beveled post cap (for more on making post caps, see the sidebar on p. 143). The tops of the posts can also be pointed by cutting a bevel on all four sides (see the photo above). Pointed posts are difficult to trim in place, so the beveling should be done before installation. In that case, you'll need to set the posts at the correct height initially.

While making the fence run parallel to grade is generally desirable, the location of a post may fall in a sudden dip in the landscape. Rather than transfer this sudden aberration in grade to the fence line, determine where to cut by pulling a string between neighboring posts. The intervening post can then be

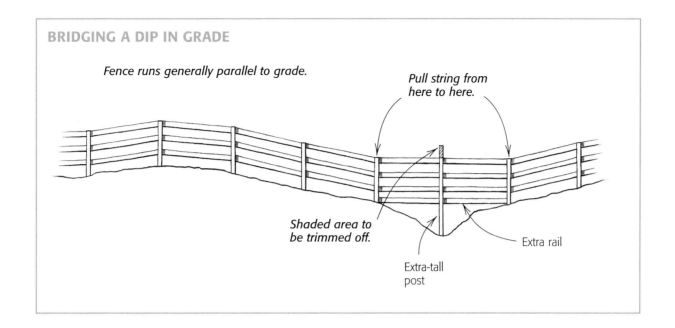

Fence runs generally parallel to grade.

Pull string from here to here.

Shaded area to be trimmed off.

Extra rail

Extra-tall post

cut off according to the line, rather than according to grade. Consequently, these special posts will be taller than the others in order to maintain a graceful line (see the drawing above).

Prefabricated panel fences cannot, by their nature, run parallel to grade. Instead, they must be installed in a stepped arrangement. To trim posts for such a fence, measure the drop in grade between neighboring post locations with a spirit level and straightedge. The process is similar to gauging variations in post–hole depth (see the drawing on p. 118). Add the drop–in–grade distance to the standard post height, plus a little extra for trimming, to find the length of each post.

Marking rails

After trimming the posts, make a measuring stick from a smooth, slender board. Let one end of the stick represent finish grade. Cut off the other end so that the stick's length equals the height of a standard post above grade. Then mark lines to represent the positions of the rails. An X indicates which side of the mark the rail will go on.

Stand the stick up next to each post and transfer your marks to the post (see the drawings on p. 146). If any extra–tall posts have been installed, as mentioned previously, you should use the tops of the neighboring posts as a reference when laying out the rails, rather than using grade as a reference.

Attaching rails

Fence rails may be fitted between posts and toenailed or simply face–nailed to one side of the post. Fitting rails between posts is more difficult, because the rails must be cut to fit tightly and because toenailing is tricky. For these reasons, installing the rail between posts is generally reserved for more formal styles, such as picket fences.

There are three basic methods of installing rails between posts (see the

Use a layout stick to establish the height of the posts and the spacing of the rails. Where sudden dips or rises occur, use a string (see the drawing on p. 145) as the reference point on the post instead of grade.

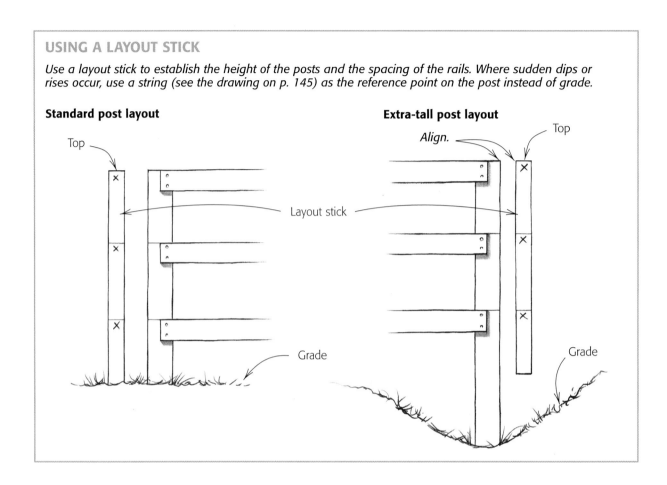

Standard post layout

Top

Layout stick

Grade

Extra-tall post layout

Align.

Top

Layout stick

Grade

drawings on p. 147). To make it a little easier, cut a shallow notch in the post (for more on notching, see p. 43). Notching posts is time–consuming, but it provides a solid bearing surface for the rail, makes nailing easier, and allows for a bit of error in the length of the rail. It's also a lot stronger than a plain toenailed joint. Metal fence brackets can also be used to connect rails to posts without toenailing. The resulting joint is very strong, if not terribly beautiful.

On most fences, rails are simply nailed to the sides of posts, but nailing correctly is important. Nailing close to the end of a rail can cause it to split, and the split worsens over time, with the weight of the rail hanging on these nails. The best way to avoid this problem is to drill pilot holes through the rails a little bit smaller than the diameter of the nail. A cordless drill works great for this. Predrilling also makes nailing easier and more accurate. The hard, stringy grain of PT yellow pine, in particular, tends to deflect nails off course without pilot holes.

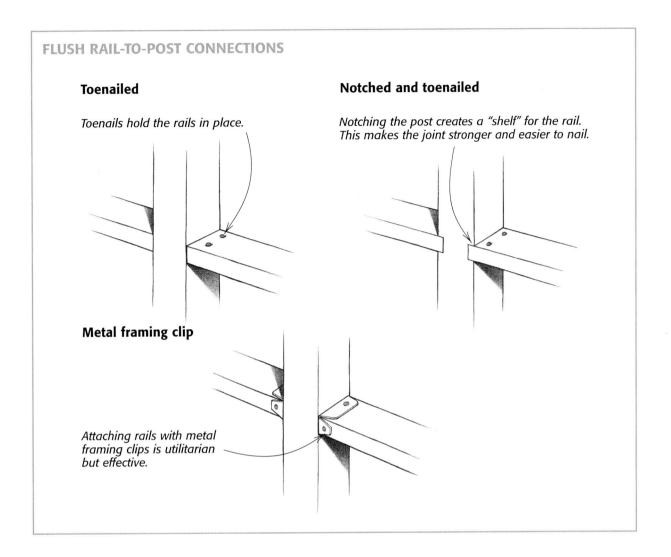

FLUSH RAIL-TO-POST CONNECTIONS

Toenailed

Toenails hold the rails in place.

Notched and toenailed

Notching the post creates a "shelf" for the rail. This makes the joint stronger and easier to nail.

Metal framing clip

Attaching rails with metal framing clips is utilitarian but effective.

Attaching pickets

If you're building a picket fence, install the pickets after the rails are on. Nail on the first picket, then check it with a level to make sure it's plumb. For standard ³/₄-in.-thick pickets, use 6d common nails, two at the top and two at the bottom. To maintain a constant distance between the top of the picket and the edge of the top rail, either measure with a ruler or make a gauge block. The block simply sits on top of the rail to guide you in setting the picket. You can make a separate gauge block to indicate the spacing between pickets or combine the two gauges (see the drawing on p. 148).

Every so often, use a level to check the last picket installed for plumb. If it's out of plumb, compensate slightly over the next several pickets until you're back on track. The eye won't readily detect minor deviations from plumb, but a sudden change of spacing to make a

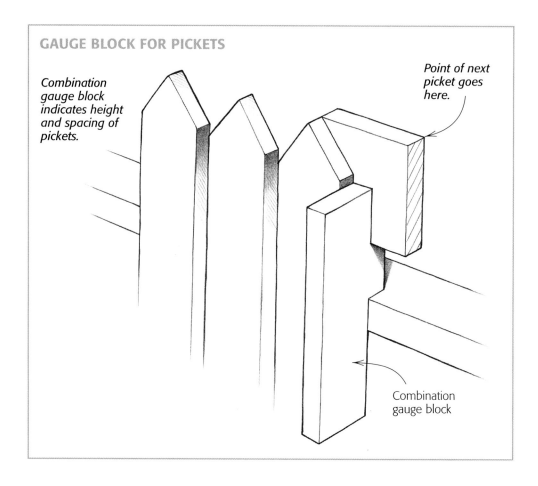

GAUGE BLOCK FOR PICKETS

Combination gauge block indicates height and spacing of pickets.

Point of next picket goes here.

Combination gauge block

correction will stand out. Keep the bottoms of the pickets at least 4 in. above grade to keep them out of the dew and to permit a string trimmer to pass underneath when cutting grass.

It's best to terminate each run of fence with a full picket, so keep this in mind as you approach the end of a run. To determine if you need to modify your spacing to ensure a full picket, cut a layout stick about 6 ft. long, hold the stick next to the pickets you have already installed, and mark off their positions. Holding this stick against the unfinished portion of the fence will tell you where the pickets will fall at your

current spacing. You can then figure out whether you should tighten the spacing or open it up a little.

Finishing a fence

In naturalized settings, no finish will be required. All woods eventually turn a silvery gray, which fits well with most landscapes. On the other hand, fences close to a home may require a paint or stain to harmonize with existing structures. You can apply the finish with a brush, roller, or spray (for more on finishes, see pp. 38–41).

Picket fences are probably the best known and loved fences. These instructions are for your basic picket fence, but you can dress it up in a number of ways. Try changing the shape of the pickets, their height, or their spacing. Adding post finials can spice up the design as well.

Whatever your particular style, you can use this basic plan to build your own picket fence. It's really easy. If you keep the pickets close together and space them

evenly, your fence will turn out fine. You can simplify the construction by nailing the rails to the outside of the posts rather than running them between posts, but the appearance won't be quite as neat.

Don't paint the posts where they show between the pickets, or at least paint them a dark color. You want it to look like there's a space between the pickets, and painting the post the same color as the fence will cause the pickets to run together visually.

(continued on page 150)

1 Dig the corner post holes with a post-hole digger. In tough soil, use a digging bar to loosen dirt, shear through roots, and dislodge stones.

2 Set and brace the corner posts, then tie a stringline between the corner posts to position the intermediate posts.

3 Measure off the locations of the intermediate posts with a tape measure and mark them with lime. After digging the holes, set each post. Nudge them close to the stringline, using a 2x4 as a lever. Leave a ¼-in. gap between the stringline and all the posts to avoid accumulated error.

4 Pack concrete around the posts and agitate it with a stick to eliminate voids. A fairly stiff mix will support the post best.

5 Trim the tops of the posts after the concrete has hardened. Stretch a stringline between the corner posts to mark the cuts.

6 Use a layout stick to mark the locations of the bottom rails, then toenail the bottom rails to the posts.

7 Make the picket points with a chopsaw. Fasten a stop block to the bench (at right) to regulate the length of the picket and to avoid repeated measurements.

8 Use a gauge block to regulate both the spacing and the height of pickets as you nail them to the rails.

10 Gates

A gate can make a strong opening statement about a home and its occupants. "Power" gates for the rich and famous, simple gates for the country cottager, and eccentric gates for the artistic are just a few of the options. Whatever the fence says, the gate should say it with an exclamation point. In addition to style, transparency is an issue on which the fence and the gate should agree. A see-through picket fence calls for a similarly friendly entrance, while a solid panel fence or a stone wall wants the guarded opacity of a solid gate or an open gate with thick, heavy members.

A gate is more than just the aesthetic focal point of a fence. It's also the fence's hardest working part. Meanwhile, only one side of the gate is supported, while the other side hangs in midair. You might say a gate has to do twice the work of an ordinary fence panel with only half the support. Gaining an understanding of the stresses at work on gates and gateposts will help you build a solid gate that will stand the test of time.

The formal elegance of this Chippendale gate speaks of aristocracy.

Cordless drills are ideal for landscape carpentry, where electricity is often beyond reach. A good cordless drill is an expensive investment, but no other power tool will get more use around your home and garden.

Every few years, a new generation of cordless drills arrives that is more powerful and longer-running than the last—18 volts is the top dog at present. You'll appreciate the extra power and running time of the heavy-duty models if you're boring large-diameter holes or driving long screws. To avoid a work stoppage when the battery runs down, it's a good idea to have an extra battery on hand. One battery recharges while the other one works.

Most cordless drills have an adjustable clutch to regulate the tool's torque (twisting power). If screw heads are snapping off as they're being tightened, reduce the clutch setting. If a drill bogs down or a screw won't drive, increase the setting for more "oomph."

In addition to the clutch setting, torque is also controlled by speed range. Most drills have a high-speed/low-torque setting and a low-speed/high-torque setting. (Actual speed varies within these ranges according to trigger pressure.) Use the high-speed range for drilling small holes, and the low-speed range for drilling large-diameter holes and for driving screws.

TYPES OF GATES

The simplest type of gate has flat horizontal rails and diagonal braces fastened to vertical pickets. Any flat board used to tie other boards together in this fashion is called a cleat, so this type of gate is known as "cleated" (see the left drawing on p. 154). The cleats should be fastened with plenty of screws, but you can substitute clinched nails for screws if you want a rough-looking gate. Plain nailing will be ineffective here because the flat pickets won't provide enough meat for the nails to sink into.

The other common way to build a gate is by constructing a frame and then covering the frame with pickets. This is called a framed, or box, gate (see the

This cottage gate welcomes the humblest pilgrim, muddy boots and all.

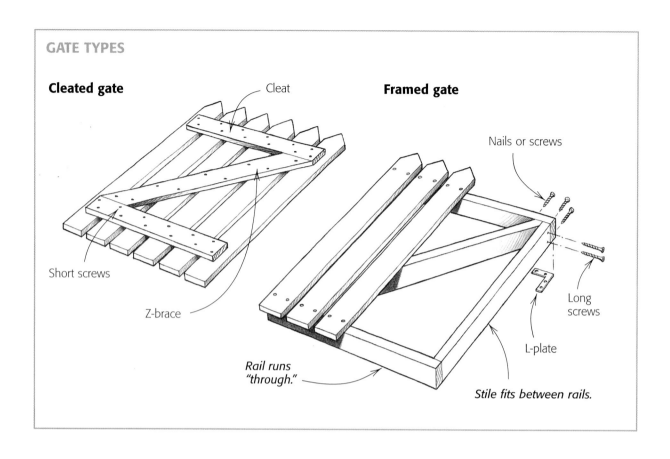

Cleated gate

Cleat

Framed gate

Nails or screws

Short screws

Z-brace

Long
screws

L-plate

*Rail runs
"through."*

Stile fits between rails.

right drawing above). Frame members are usually butted together, with the stiles (vertical members) fitted in between the top and bottom rails. Because a frame has ample thickness, you can use nails to fasten the pickets to the frame instead of screws. But you should use long, coarse–thread screws to secure the corner joints for maximum strength. Also, attach galvanized steel L–plates to the corners, because even screws have limited strength when dri–ven into end grain. Braces should fit snug within the frame and be fastened with long screws as well. A framed gate requires more labor and material than a cleated gate, but the finished product feels heftier and has a more substantial look (a photo essay on building a framed gate begins on p. 163).

GATE CONSTRUCTION

To meet the aesthetic and functional requirements of a good gate, it's wise to invest in some careful planning. An accurate scale drawing is essential for working out the details of your gate design. If the gate has a unique infill pattern, make a full–scale rendering on a sheet of plywood, then transfer the cut–ting angles for the various members directly from the sheet to the pieces being cut.

It's a good idea to buy your gate hardware and have it in front of you as you work out the design. The reasons for this are both aesthetic and practical. For instance, wide strap hinges can make a strong visual statement, but they should be sized carefully in proportion to the gate. Meanwhile, different types of latches and hinges mount in different ways. The choice of hardware can also have an effect on the clearance between the gate and gatepost. You don't want any surprises after you've constructed the gate.

Braces

An overriding concern in gate design is diagonal bracing. Because gates are sup-ported on the hinge side only, the unsupported latch side tends to sag. The wider a gate is in relation to its height, the greater the strain will be because the weight of the latch side is amplified through leverage. You can combat the problem of sagging in a variety of ways, depending on the gate style. Cleated gates may not need a brace, as long as you use wide rails (8 in. or wider) and plenty of fasteners to maximize their grip on a comparatively small area.

The most common solution for sag-ging is a Z-brace (see the drawings at right). If the Z-brace runs from the top of the latch side to the bottom of the hinge side, the brace is in compression. If the brace runs from the bottom of the latch side to the top of the hinge side, the brace is in tension. There is a pre-vailing opinion that wooden gate braces work better in compression than in ten-sion because that arrangement throws more weight against the bottom of the gatepost, where the post is strongest. However, either arrangement works, as long as all the members are joined securely together.

A Z-brace that runs from corner to corner gives maximum support and should always be used for wide gates. Narrower gates can be adequately stiff-ened with shorter braces running between adjacent sides, opening up the

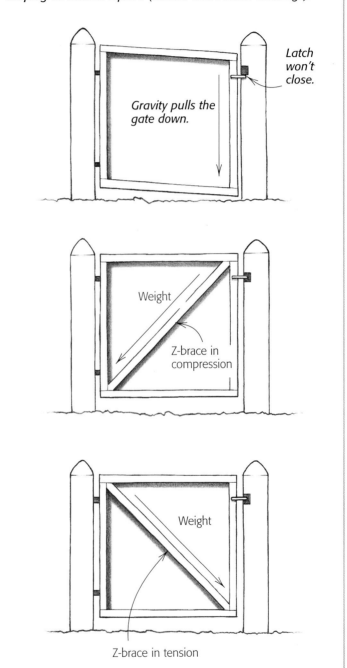

BRACING A GATE

Gravity causes an unbraced gate to sag (top drawing). Adding some sort of diagonal bracing will stiffen the gate, keeping its corners square (middle and bottom drawings).

Latch won't close.

Gravity pulls the gate down.

Weight

Z-brace in compression

Weight

Z-brace in tension

The braces on this gate turn out with a subtle flare. The result is a country gate with panache.

A cross buck in the lower half of each gate provides good bracing. Pickets in the upper half permit a glimpse of the home beyond.

middle of the gate for other design possibilities. Just be sure that when you add a brace it's diagonal; vertical and horizontal members won't stiffen the gate.

Braces don't have to be straight. A gently curved brace will do most of the work of a straight brace, as long as it's not too narrow (see the left photo above). A narrow curving brace, however, is apt to split because its contoured edges cut across the grain of the wood.

If the look of a solid brace is objectionable, use a slender wire brace in conjunction with a turnbuckle. If the gate sags, you can simply tighten the turnbuckle to bring the gate back into squareness. Because wire has plenty of tensile strength but no compressive strength, wire braces must run from the top of the hinge side to the bottom of the latch side. You can use aircraft cable to make a wire brace or a slender rod-and-

turnbuckle brace made specifically for screen doors. The rod-and-turnbuckle type has the neater appearance, but it may be too long for your gate. To shorten the rod, cut it with a hacksaw. Once the length is right, hammer the end of the rod on a hard surface to flatten it and drill screw holes through the flattened end.

For a solid gate, consider running infill boards diagonally for stiffness to avoid the need for bracing. You can also glue a wide plywood panel into a gate to prevent sagging. Plywood doesn't hold up well in exposed locations, but for gates with some sort of roof or covering arch, plywood is a good choice. Be sure to use pressure-treated (PT) or marine-grade plywood to protect the gate from wind-driven rain. Groove the unsightly edges of the panel into the stiles and rails or conceal them behind stop moldings.

You can enliven solid gates by cutting out portions of the covering material, be it solid boards or plywood. Light shining through the cutouts will contrast sharply with the surrounding surface, especially if the solid area is a dark color. When making cutouts in plywood, be sure to use a very fine-toothed blade because plywood surface veneers splinter easily.

If you want the benefits of both an open and a solid gate, consider a half-and-half design, with solid infill below and spaced pickets or lattice above. The upper section affords transparency where it's most important—looking toward the horizon—while the lower panel provides stiffness. For strength, the lower section is sometimes reinforced with a cross buck—a pair of crossed framing members running between opposing corners (see the right photo on the facing page).

If your gate design won't abide any type of bracing, you'll be depending entirely on the rigidity of the gate's corner joints. One joinery method, known as mortise and tenon, is so strong that it can support gates with little or no bracing (depending on the width of the gate). Unfortunately, mortise-and-tenon joints are beyond the skills and equipment of most amateurs. If you want this type of gate but lack the skills to build it, consult a cabinetmaker about building it for you.

Gateposts

Gateposts have a constant strain imposed upon them by the weight of the gate. When the gate is closed, this weight is transferred to the adjoining fence. When the gate is swung open, however, the weight of the gate wants to pull the post sideways. To counteract this tendency, a gatepost needs to be planted deeper—and be more solidly backfilled—than a regular fence post. In the case of a very wide or heavy gate, the gatepost may need to be increased in thickness as well. Otherwise, the gatepost is liable to bend at ground level, causing the gate to sag and, eventually, to drag on the ground.

Dig holes for gateposts at least 3 ft. deep. For gates wider than 3 ft., dig the holes as deep as the gate is wide, or as deep as you can reach with the equipment at your disposal (for more on digging post holes, see p. 52–55). Hang gates up to 3 ft. wide on 4-in.-thick posts, gates up to 5 ft. wide on 6-in.-thick posts, and wider gates on 8-in.-thick posts. Increasing the height of a gatepost can give better leverage to the brace, but it places even greater strain on the post (see the photo on p. 158), so be sure to use a stout post.

The diameter of a gatepost hole should be larger than for a fence post for better anchorage, and the hole should be backfilled with concrete. If the hole isn't large enough, the hardened concrete plug surrounding the gatepost is apt to cut through the soil when the gatepost is strained. Make the gatepost hole at least four times the thickness of the post.

To make a gate more stylish, you can hang it on painted hollow box posts. A box post made from seasoned boards won't develop surface checks like a solid unseasoned post will. The corners of a box post should be glued and nailed well with finish nails. Screws are even stronger, but they will need to be

The height of this gatepost affords good leverage to the brace. The stoutness of the post enables it to withstand the extra strain exerted on the post by this arrangement.

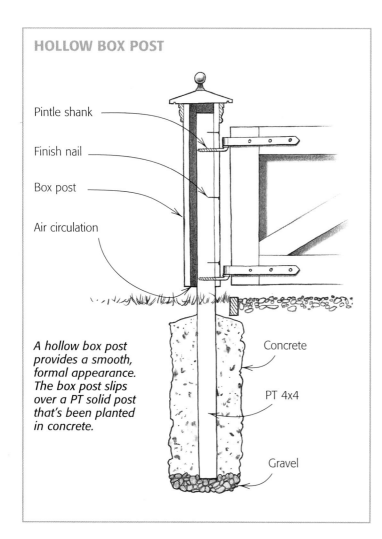

HOLLOW BOX POST

Pintle shank

Finish nail

Box post

Air circulation

A hollow box post provides a smooth, formal appearance. The box post slips over a PT solid post that's been planted in concrete.

Concrete

PT 4x4

Gravel

plugged for appearance's sake (for more on plugging screw holes, see the sidebar on the facing page).

Properly constructed box posts have almost as much strength as solid posts of the same size. However, it isn't wise to set a box post below grade because moisture from the ground will get inside and cause it to decay quicker. The solution is to bury a PT solid post and then slip the hollow box post over it (see the drawing at left). Make the inside dimensions of the box post greater than the outside dimensions of the solid post for a comfortable fit. When installing the gate, make sure the hinges are fastened *through* the box post into the solid post for support. Leave an airspace between the bottom of the box post and the ground to keep water from wicking into the box post's end-grain and to allow some air to circulate inside.

Hardware

The choice of gate hardware at most hardware stores leans toward the functional-but-ugly types made of stamped, galvanized steel. If you are going to the trouble of building a custom gate, you might consider purchasing wrought-iron hardware instead. It's harder to find and a lot more expensive than stamped hardware but much better looking. If there are any blacksmiths in your area, they may be able to forge custom hardware to your specifications.

Hinges No matter what type of gate you choose to build, it needs to swing on a set of hinges. So let's take a look at the three most common gate hinges (see the drawings on p. 160): butt hinges, T-hinges, and pintle hinges.

Butt hinges are the square hinges typically used to hang house doors. You

Plugging Screw Holes

To plug a screw hole, begin by drilling a counterbore (a hole about ⅛ in. larger than the screw head) in the piece being fastened. The depth of the counterbore should be about one-third the thickness of the board. After drilling the counterbore, finish drilling through the board with a bit whose diameter is smaller than the head of the screw but larger than the screw's shank.

After the screw is installed, glue a wooden plug into the counterbore, leaving the top of the plug slightly above the surface (a condition known as proud). When the glue has dried, plane off the excess wood to within a shaving's thickness and then sand the plug flush.

You can buy wooden plugs from mail-order woodworking catalogs and good hardware stores. You can also buy a tool called a plug cutter for making your own wood plugs. The plug cutter is a sort of hollow drill bit that fits in a drill press and is driven into a board to produce a

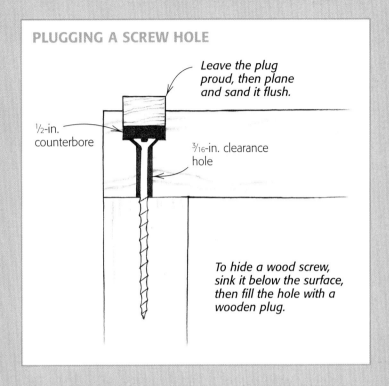

PLUGGING A SCREW HOLE

Leave the plug proud, then plane and sand it flush.

½-in. counterbore

³⁄₁₆-in. clearance hole

To hide a wood screw, sink it below the surface, then fill the hole with a wooden plug.

plug of a given size. One of the nice things about making your own plugs is that you can use a decay-resistant wood for exterior work.

can easily mount the leaves of a butt hinge on the face of a gate, but a neater look is achieved by mounting the leaves on the edge of the gate and the side of the gatepost. When the gate is closed, only the barrel of the hinge will show. If you desire a very tight fit between the post and the gate, recess the leaves into the surfaces of the gate and post with a chisel or router. The recess will also help support the hinge. Since the permissible

clearance around a gate is greater than that for a door, recessing the hinge leaves isn't necessary.

T–hinges have one rectangular leaf and one long tapered leaf. The rectangular leaf is usually mounted to either the face or the edge of the gatepost, and the long tapered leaf mounts on the face of the gate. T–hinges are the easiest of all hinges to install—just wedge the gate into position, hold the hinge in place,

Butt hinge

Butt hinges can be face mounted or edge mounted. For a tight fit, the leaves of the hinge can be recessed flush with the wood's surface.

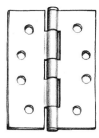

T-hinge

T-hinges are easy to apply. The rectangular leaf is usually mounted on the gatepost, while the tapered leaf is mounted on the gate.

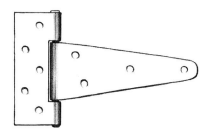

Pintle hinge

Pintle hinges can be mounted on round gateposts as well as square ones. The type shown has a lag-threaded shank, but machine-threaded versions are also available. Straps can be fancy, such as this heart-tipped pattern, or plain.

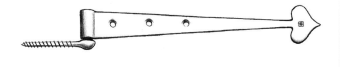

A hand-forged iron gate latch harmonizes with this weathered oak gate.

and drive in the screws. When setting the wedges, cock the gate a little toward the gatepost at the top to compensate for the looseness between the hinge's pin and barrel (see the bottom drawing on the facing page). When you remove the wedges, the gate will settle into a level position.

Pintle hinges are very versatile. They can be mounted on round posts as well as on square ones. The pintle is a vertical pin on the end of a horizontal shank. The shank usually has a coarse thread similar to a lag bolt, and the shank can be threaded into the face or side of a gatepost. If the pintle is mounted on the side, the gate can be made to swing both in and out, although this requires extra clearance between the post and the gate to keep the corners of the gate from rubbing against the post. Rounding the edges of the gate reduces the necessary clearance. Be sure to work out the clearance carefully before measuring for the gate.

The other half of a pintle hinge is the part that mounts on the gate. A strap is most common, sometimes terminating in a decorative heart or bean shape, and it is generally bolted to the gate. A U-shaped strap is available that straddles both sides of a gate, making it well suited to swinging in both directions. Other types of pintle hinges employ a lag-threaded eye or a machine-threaded eye, which make the hinges adjustable. If the gate sags, you can change the position of the eye relative to the gate, either by backing out a lag-threaded shank or by adjusting the jam nuts on a machine-threaded shank.

Latches There are a few types of gate latches available, from simple to not so simple (see the top drawings at right). The typical gate latch consists of a latch bar (or latch pin) and a keeper (or striker). In some versions, the latch bar pivots up and down, settling into a fixed keeper. In other versions, the latch pin is fixed, but the keeper opens and closes. Mounting either of these is a matter of holding the parts in position, marking the screw holes, and driving the screws.

The slide bolt is similarly straightforward. The bolt slides horizontally, fitting into a keeper or sleeve. A pivot-type latch has an advantage over a slide bolt because it latches itself when shut, whereas a slide bolt requires locking and unlocking. Pivot-type latches also have some built-in tolerance for misalignment should the gate sag, while slide bolts do not.

A cane bolt is used to hold double gates in position, such as in the middle of a driveway. The bolt slides into a pipe or a block of wood set flush in the road bed. Both halves of the gate can be fixed

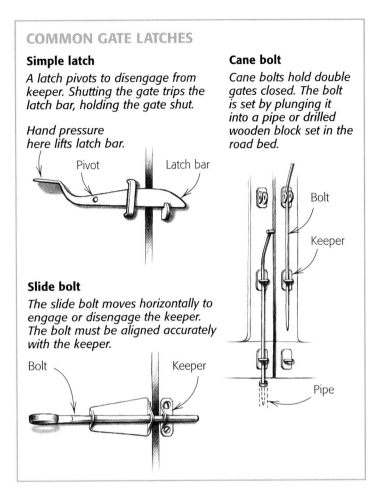

COMMON GATE LATCHES

Simple latch
A latch pivots to disengage from keeper. Shutting the gate trips the latch bar, holding the gate shut.

Hand pressure here lifts latch bar.

Pivot   Latch bar

Cane bolt
Cane bolts hold double gates closed. The bolt is set by plunging it into a pipe or drilled wooden block set in the road bed.

Bolt

Keeper

Pipe

Slide bolt
The slide bolt moves horizontally to engage or disengage the keeper. The bolt must be aligned accurately with the keeper.

Bolt   Keeper

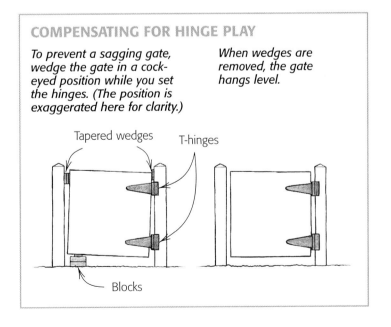

COMPENSATING FOR HINGE PLAY

To prevent a sagging gate, wedge the gate in a cock-eyed position while you set the hinges. (The position is exaggerated here for clarity.)

When wedges are removed, the gate hangs level.

Tapered wedges   T-hinges

Blocks

GATE CLOSERS

Spring closer

A spring closer uses spring tension to close the gate automatically.

Cannonball closer

A cannonball closer uses gravity to shut the gate.

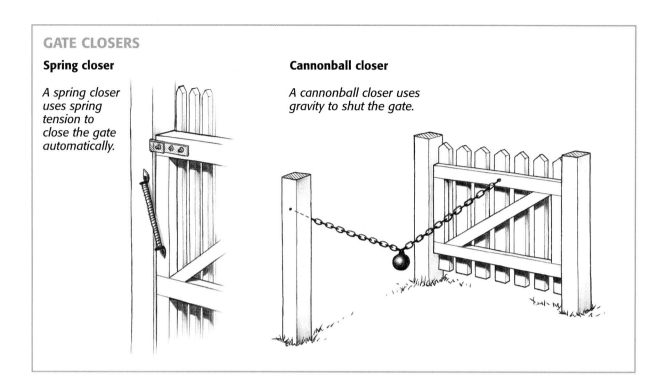

with cane bolts, or one half can be latched to the other (cane–bolted) half.

A mortise latch has a mechanism that's recessed into the edge of the gate stile. Mounting a mortise latch is considerably more work than mounting any kind of surface–mounted latch, but the result is a very neat look.

There are also some very simple ways of latching a gate that don't require much hardware or effort. A bail is a semicircular band, cord, or wire that flips over the top of a gatepost to capture a gate stile or picket. A chain and clip does much the same thing. The chain is fastened to the gatepost, loops around the gate somehow, and its end is then clipped or hooked onto an eye set on the post. These retainers are very forgiving of misalignment, so they're often

used for rough agricultural gates. The hook and eye is another device that isn't too fussy about the gate's fit. A hook hung on the gate slips into an eye set on the post (or vice versa). One type of heavy-duty hook has a spring-loaded jaw that must be retracted for the hook to release from the eye.

Closers A gate that closes by itself is desirable when kids or pets are forbidden to pass (see the drawings above). The spring–loaded butt hinges made for screen doors work fine for small gates. You can also find a heavy-duty spring closer that straddles the hinge stile and gatepost. Perhaps the classiest member of this category is the cannonball closer, which hails from Colonial Williamsburg.

The pickets in this gate are nailed to a sturdy 2x4 frame. You can achieve a lighter gate simply by screwing the pickets to a set of cleats. The tops of the pickets are arranged here in a shieldlike design that's reminiscent of a gothic arch. A similar shape is used to detail the pickets themselves. To simplify the design, you could use spear-point pickets topped straight across, but it's easy to build as is. Another decorative feature of this gate is the asymmetrical arrangement of the braces. There are three braces instead of the typical one or two, which adds strength as well as a chevron motif.

The key to building a strong gate—framed or cleated—is to be sure the braces are well fastened to prevent sagging. Screws are the best fasteners for that job. This particular gate is hung on stone piers, but it could also be hung on wood posts. I reused the hardware that was on the original gate because it was built into the stone piers, but for a wood post, you would probably use butt hinges or T-hinges. I didn't put a closer on this gate, but you could easily add one.

(continued on page 164)

1 Assemble a rectangular frame of 2x4s with screws. You can use pipe clamps to hold the pieces together during assembly.

2 Check corner-to-corner measurements to make sure that the frame is square, then scribe a corner brace to fit its intended location. Screw corner braces into the frame. Check the frame for square one more time before installing pickets.

3 Nail oversize pickets to the frame.

4 Use a trammel stick to scribe a pair of wide arcs that intersect at the top of the middle picket (see p. 116). You'll have to find the length of the trammel and the correct center points by trial and error.

5 Use a template to mark the tops of the pickets. Hold the point of the template to the previously scribed arcs.

6 Use a jigsaw to trim the pickets to shape.

7 An inverted pintle bolt, salvaged from the previous gate, is used here to hang the new gate on a stone pier. To hang the gate on a wood post, set the pintle upright in the post instead, and mount a threaded eye on the gate stile. To drill a hole for the bolt, slip the pintle into its pivot hole and indicate the position of the bolt on the face of the gate stile. Use a square to transfer the bolt location from the face of the stile to the stile's centerline before drilling. Place a wooden shim block under the gate during marking to ensure that the gate will clear the walk after the gate is hung.

8 To adjust the gate sideways, tighten one jam nut while the other is slacked off. You can plumb a cock-eyed gate by adjusting one pintle or the other in this fashion. If a lag-threaded eye had been used here instead, it could have been similarly adjusted by backing out or driving in its shank.

Resources

PRESSURE-TREATED LUMBER

Kodiak, Inc.
PO Box 9158
416 E. Brooks Rd.
Memphis, TN 38109
(800) K–KODIAK
www.kodiakwood.com
CDDC-treated lumber (CDDC is a preservative that imparts a brown color instead of the green color associated with CCA)

Mellco
906 Ball St.
Perry, GA 31069
(800) 866–1414, Fax (800) 777–3299
www.mellco.com
CCA-treated lumber

Quality Forest Products
Rt. 1, Box 406QF
Enfield, NC 27823
(800) 617–5461
ACQ-treated lumber

ENGINEERED LUMBER

Gruen–Wald Engineered Laminates
220 S. Marion Rd.
Sioux Falls, SD 57107
(605) 338–8004
Laminated posts

Rigidply Rafters
701 E. Linden St.
Richland, PA 17087
(717) 866–6581
Laminated arches and beams

Trex Company
20 S. Cameron St.
Winchester, VA 22601
(800) 289–8739
www.trex.com
Wood-polymer lumber

Trus Joist MacMillan
200 E. Mallard Dr.
Boise, ID 83706
(800) 628–3997
Parallel-strand lumber

TROPICAL HARDWOOD LUMBER

Good Wood Alliance
PO Box 1525
Burlington, VT 05402–1525
www.goodwood.org/goodwood/index.html
Source directory of sustainably harvested lumber

Plunkett Webster, Inc.
2 Clinton Pl.
New Rochelle, NY 10801
(914) 636–8770, Fax (914) 636–4477
Mahogany

Timber Holdings, Ltd.
2400 W. Cornell St.
Milwaukee, WI 53209
(414) 445–8989, Fax (414) 445–9155
www.ironwoods.com
Assorted tropical hardwoods

Tree Talk
PO Box 426
Burlington, VT 05402
(802) 863–6789
www.forestworld.com
*Descriptions of over 900 species of wood
on compact disk*

PREFABRICATED FENCES AND GARDEN STRUCTURES

Anderson Design/Garden Arches
PO Box 4057
Bellingham, WA 98227
(360) 650–1587, Fax (360) 650–0733

Ryther–Purdy Lumber Co., Inc.
174 Elm St.
PO Box 622
Old Saybrook, CT 06475
(860) 388–4405, Fax (860) 388–9401
www.ek-designs.com\Rytherpurdy

Walpole Woodworkers
767 East St. (Rt. 27)
Walpole, MA 02081
(800) 343–6948, Fax (508) 668–7301
Also sells gate hardware

GATE HARDWARE

Historic Housefitters Co.
509 Rte. 312
P.O. Box 26
Brewster, NY 10509
(800) 247–4111, Fax (914) 278–7726

Horton Brasses, Inc.
PO Box 95
Nooks Hill Rd.
Cromwell, CT 06416
(800) 754–9127, Fax (860) 635–6473

Kayne & Son Custom Hardware, Inc.
100 Daniel Ridge Rd.
Candler, NC 28715
(704) 667–8868, Fax (828) 665–8303

Whitechapel, Ltd.
PO Box 136
Wilson, WY 83014
(800) 468–5534, Fax (307) 739–9458

Williamsburg Blacksmiths
PO Box 1776
Rt. 9
Williamsburg, MA 01096
(800) 248–1776, Fax (413) 268–9317

Index

Publisher: JIM CHILDS

Associate publisher: HELEN ALBERT

Editorial assistant: CHERILYN DeVRIES

Editors: JENNIFER RENJILIAN, THOMAS MCKENNA,
RUTH HAMEL

Designer/layout artist: ROSALIE VACCARO

Photographer except where noted: SCOTT McBRIDE

Illustrator: MICHAEL GELLATLY

Indexer: HARRIET HODGES